Snitching for Personal Gain:

Secrets Exposed From The Inside

Marcus Watkins

Contents

Prologue

I was born in Atlanta, Georgia on April 6, 1971 to a beautiful child of 15 years of age. Born to my biological mother, she wasn't ready to parent and nurture me as a mother, so I was immediately placed in the custody of her parents, whom, from my recollection, were my loving, wonderful grandparents. My other parent? — I know of him, but he was never a father to me and has never been a post-pregnancy contributor, nor a factor in my life.

Although not my biological parents, my grandparents have always been considered my true parents. Categorically, being raised by them was the best thing that ever happened to me, and I will cherish and hold that experience dear to my heart for the rest of my life. I couldn't have asked for better parenting. Don't get me wrong, they were not perfect people, as we all fall short, but they were perfect for me.

The imperfection of my grandparents' environment brought me in contact with all types of hustlers, i.e. individuals of the criminal element at a very early age. My grandfather and his sons were all hustlers in one way or another, which ultimately led me down Hustler's Avenue as well. Whereas my grandfather's hustle was an illegal numbers operation, by the time I had reached the age of 16 in 1987, my uncles on my mother's side of the family and one of my uncles on my biological father's side of the family had exposed me to a shorter but dirty path to making money plus a fast and dangerous lifestyle, "The Drug Game." In this book, I will make dramatic reference to the arrest of that uncle, my father's brother.

By the time that I entered the Atlanta drug game in 1987 at 16, my mother was already heavily addicted to crack cocaine. During a drug transaction that I was conducting within her apartment, she actually tried to entice me to smoke crack cocaine. She was the first of several individuals that tried to get me to smoke crack cocaine. Even though I refused to take a hit of her crack pipe initially, we would indeed smoke crack cocaine together on numerous occasions later in life.

Shortly after entering the drug game, I went to many social events and gatherings held by older women, which led to me having sex with a few of them, snorting a hell of a lot of cocaine, and smoking sticks of marijuana laced with crack cocaine, to fit in.

Eighteen months after my introduction to the short path of fast money, I found myself addicted to crack cocaine which I have yet to recover from. Growing up as a kid in that type of environment, not in my wildest nightmare would I have ever imagined that my life would come to this: Hood glamour, fast women, tricked out cars, a shit load of money, and a dope-ass crib, a'ight. But this? — No way!

For the 13 years since October 2006, I, federal detainee Marcus A. Watkins #46440-019, have been in Federal custody without being sentenced (Federal Court case no.1:06-CR-442-TCB-AJB). With 6 years and 4 months of that 13 years confined to a cell on 24 hours a day lock-down, "Involuntary Protective Custody" housing status, meaning no normal activity (See Exhibit A-2) of the prologue. Inside of the B-5 Segregation Housing Unit of the Robert A. Deyton Detention Facility (RADDF-Deyton), located in Lovejoy, Georgia, my need to be housed on "Involuntary Protective Custody" housing status was at the discretion of the facility's warden, Ralph Cherry.

This was the direct result of a December 14, 2012 front page USA Today article entitled, "Federal Prisoners Use Snitching for Personal Gain," which has since placed my life in grave danger (See Exhibit A-1). Prior to its publication, I was being housed amongst the detainees in the general population; however, since the USA Today's extraordinary news flash, I have received numerous threats from other detainees housed at the facility. I have even been the targeted victim of violent, conspired, staff involved physical assault, resulting in serious injury.

My hope is that you will be enlightened to the real world of a **criminal "injustice" system and government corruption** to the point that you are careful in a world where you perceive that the government has your best interest at heart. Truthfully, they don't! Call it naivety or subtle expectation, whatever. But we often ignore or reason away that those holding titled governing positions are human and, therefore, have the ability to be criminally vindictive — **"Breaking the Law for P&P Gain — Personal & Political."** Coincidental? No! Sound familiar?

Exhibit A-1

The Telling USA TODAY Snitching Article

Federal prisoners use snitching for personal gain

Brad Heath, USA TODAY

ATLANTA – The prisoners in Atlanta's hulking downtown jail had a problem. They wanted to snitch for federal agents, but they didn't know anything worth telling.

Fellow prisoner Marcus Watkins, an armed robber, had the answer.

For a fee, Watkins and his associates on the outside sold them information about other criminals that they could turn around and offer up to federal agents in hopes of shaving years off their prison sentences. They were paying for information, but what they were really trying to buy was freedom.

"I didn't feel as though any laws were being broken," Watkins wrote in a 2008 letter to prosecutors. "I really thought I was helping out law enforcement."

"I didn't feel as though any laws were being broken," Watkins wrote in a 2008 letter to prosecutors. "I really thought I was helping out law enforcement."

That pay-to-snitch enterprise – documented in thousands of pages of court records, interviews and a stack of Watkins' own letters – remains almost entirely unknown outside Atlanta's towering federal courthouse, where investigators are still trying to determine whether any criminal cases were compromised. It offers a rare glimpse inside a vast and almost always secret part of the federal criminal justice system in which prosecutors routinely use the promise of reduced prison time to reward prisoners who help federal agents build cases against other criminals.

Snitching has become so commonplace that in the past five years at least 48,895 federal convicts — one of every eight — had their prison sentences reduced in exchange for helping government investigators, a USA TODAY examination of hundreds of thousands of court cases found. The deals can chop a decade or more off of their sentences.

How often informants pay to acquire information from brokers such as Watkins is impossible to know, in part because judges routinely seal court records that could identify them. It almost certainly represents an extreme result of a system that puts strong pressure on defendants to cooperate. Still, Watkins' case is at least the fourth such scheme to be uncovered in Atlanta alone over the past 20 years.

Those schemes are generally illegal because the people who buy information usually lie to federal agents about where they got it. They also show how staggeringly valuable good information has become – prices ran into tens of thousands of dollars, or up to $250,000 in one case, court records show.

John Horn, the second in command of Atlanta's U.S. attorney's office, said the "investigation on some of these matters is continuing" but would not elaborate.

Prosecutors have said they were troubled that informants were paying for some of the secrets they passed on to federal agents. Judges are outraged. But the inmates who operated the schemes have repeatedly alleged that agents knew all along what they were up to, and sometimes even gave them the information they sold. Prosecutors told a judge in October that an investigation found those accusations were false. Still, court records show, agents kept interviewing at least one of Watkins' customers even after the FBI learned of the scheme.

The risks are obvious. If the government rewards paid-for information, wealthy defendants could potentially buy early freedom. Because such a system further muddies the question of how informants — already widely viewed as untrustworthy — know what they claim to know, "individual cases can be undermined and the system itself is compromised," U.S. Justice Department lawyers said in a 2010 court filing.

Before Watkins became an informant, he was a prolific armed robber.

In 1995, he held up a string of shops and restaurants, sometimes robbing the same place more than once, and sometimes pulling more than one robbery a day, according to court records. The last time he was arrested, in 2006, Atlanta police said he asked a supermarket clerk for a pack of cigarettes, stepped back, pulled a handgun and yelled "robbery." He fled before he got any money, employees caught him, and federal prosecutors hit him with a gun charge that could have put him in prison for the rest of his life.

By then, Watkins had been a federal informant for a decade, he said in a letter to USA TODAY. He claimed he once wore a wire inside a prison to help catch another man who was selling information to would-be witnesses. That man, Gregory Harris, later confessed, but, in an unusual move, the government agreed to halve the 20-year prison sentence Harris was already serving in exchange for his cooperation in other cases. (Harris was found dead this year inside the trunk of a burning car.)

And so began a career of trying to cash in on what he knew.

Pressure, and plenty of cooperation

People charged with federal crimes don't have many ways to avoid a tough sentence.

Nearly everyone charged is convicted. They usually face the prospect of a lengthy prison term, driven by long minimum sentences for drug crimes and sentencing rules that leave judges little leeway to make exceptions – unless they cooperate. Often, becoming an informant is the only chance defendants have.

An experienced lawyer who knows what his client has been charged with "can ask a client three or four questions, and you can get 95% accuracy on the sentencing range within 10 minutes ... unless he has something to trade," said Tim Saviello, a John Marshall Law School professor and former federal public defender in Atlanta. "People are willing to pay $20,000 or $30,000 to get a piece of information. That tells you how valuable it is."

Every year for the past decade, 11% or more of the people convicted of a federal crime got a shorter sentence because they provided "substantial assistance" to investigators, a USA TODAY examination of federal sentencing data shows. That figure almost certainly understates the extent to which defendants cooperate because some get breaks that aren't reflected in court records and others only pass on information that the government doesn't find useful.

In return, prisoners offer up names and addresses of drug dealers. They wear recording devices or let police listen to their phone calls. They introduce undercover agents to their contacts inside crime organizations.

That kind of help has become indispensable for law enforcement. The Drug Enforcement Administration told the Justice Department's inspector general in 2005 that it "could not effectively enforce the controlled-substances laws of the United States" without its confidential sources.

Cooperation is especially common when drugs are involved. Nationwide, at least a quarter of the people sent to federal prison in drug-trafficking cases over the past five years successfully traded information for a shorter sentence. In some parts of the country – including Idaho, Colorado and western New York – more than half did, while in Nebraska, fewer than 5% of convicted drug traffickers got deals. One reason is that some prosecutors' offices demand far more cooperation to get a deal.

The benefits can be huge. Last year, half of the defendants who cooperated with the government got their sentences chopped by 50% or more, according to a U.S. Sentencing Commission report. People convicted of some white-collar crimes such as bribery and tax evasion usually avoid prison entirely.

It's up to Justice Department lawyers to decide who gets a break.

A jailhouse enterprise

Watkins' business plan was simple.

His associates on the outside collected information about drug dealers and other criminals, and he offered to sell it to other prisoners at the Atlanta City Detention Center who had money but lacked the facts or criminal contacts to cooperate with the government on their own. Sometimes the money ended up in a jail account that inmates use to buy commissary items, according to court records.

In exchange, he would deliver "packages" of information that his customers could share with federal agents looking to open new cases or buttress old ones.

The trouble was most of what Watkins had to sell was "classic street-level information" that was of little interest to federal agents looking to take down major drug traffickers, said Robert McBurney, who worked a related case when he was a federal prosecutor in Atlanta. He said Justice Department lawyers were uncomfortable shortening one prisoner's sentence as a reward for someone else's information, and doubly so when the would-be informants concealed the fact that their information was secondhand.

And then there was the money. "There were discussions that, if the information he relayed is valid, maybe he's an entrepreneur. If he chooses to get money instead of a reduction in sentence, Adam Smith would applaud that," McBurney said, invoking the 18th-century economist. But prosecutors didn't take the same view.

Watkins said he didn't see the problem. "The biggest buyer of information is the government," he said during a brief phone call from a detention center in Georgia. "But they pay in years."

He claimed during a phone call that the agents who debriefed him "knew money's been changing hands," and his lawyer said in court filings that it should have been obvious to investigators that Watkins was getting outside information. "They basically authorized all of this," Watkins said. He said he is still providing information to federal agents, an allegation that prosecutors have disputed.

Watkins' enterprise didn't come to light until the summer of 2008, when another inmate contacted prosecutors looking for a deal – with information about Watkins. (He got one.) Watkins later told the FBI that he had brokered deals for four inmates. James Rochester, the informant who turned him in – and had been intercepting his mail – told federal prosecutors through his lawyer that he thought there were at least a dozen customers. Watkins himself wrote to agents and prosecutors admitting that he had acted as a broker for other prisoners seeking information.

McBurney said prosecutors tried to review all cases that could have been tainted by Watkins' scheme. "It's a pernicious situation that, sadly, undid some good works," McBurney said. But FBI agent Mile Brosas testified in

December 2010 that agents went "just based on the names that Mr. Watkins gave us."

Neither Watkins nor his customers were ever prosecuted for the scheme. At least one actually won a reduced sentence.

Watkins is still angling to get his own sentence reduced.

He pleaded guilty to a federal gun charge in 2007; in exchange, the government promised in a written plea agreement to recommend a 30-year sentence. But five and a half years later, he still hasn't been sentenced. Part of the reason is that he's still trying to get a judge to force the Justice Department to give him a "substantial assistance" reduction as a reward for the help he said he has given to state and federal agents.

The Justice Department "feigns dismay that Marcus Watkins was allegedly buying and selling information when the Government had been legally buying information from him over a lengthy period of time," his lawyer, Martin Cowen III, alleged in one court filing. He said it should have been obvious to agents by 2008 that Watkins – who had been in prison for two years by then – couldn't have been giving them current information about criminals unless he was getting it from someone outside the jail.

The government, Cowen said, was "'shocked, shocked' to find that information was being sold in the jail."

But if prosecutors weren't actually surprised, Atlanta's chief federal judge was. At a hearing in 2010, U.S. District Court Judge Julie Carnes excoriated the "abominable situation" of prisoners trading for outside information, and said she was "appalled that it's going on to the level it appears to be going on." The scheme, she said, could let the wealthy buy their way to reduced sentences, conjuring images of Hessian mercenaries of the Revolutionary War.

Carnes still hasn't decided what to do with Watkins.

Information has a price

Watkins' enterprise wasn't the only time someone here figured out how much information was worth.

In 2010, federal prosecutors indicted another man, Sandeo Dyson — an Army medic locked up on charges that he had tried to burn down a strip club for money — for running a similar scheme out of the same jail at the same time as Watkins. His customers paid $5,000 and $10,000 for information they hoped would win them lighter sentences. Prosecutors said he made $50,000 selling information to four other inmates.

Dyson pleaded guilty to a charge of encouraging his customers to lie to agents about the source of their information and was sentenced to 18 more months in prison.

U.S. District Judge Richard Story had planned to lock Dyson up longer. But by the time Dyson's attorney, Barry Lombardo, finished sketching the history of the pay-to-snitch business in Atlanta, Story instead sentenced him to the bottom end of what the federal sentencing guidelines said was appropriate, Lombardo said. (The transcript of that hearing remains sealed.)

In 2000, prosecutors here convicted Harris.

Four years before that, agents charged a prominent local defense lawyer, Robert Fierer, and his former drug-dealer client, Kevin Pappas, with running an even bigger information-for-sale enterprise. Their customers were quoted prices up to $250,000 for information that they hoped might help them go home sooner, according to court records.

To get a deal, Pappas said, people needed the right kind of information about the right kind of criminal – solid information about someone significant enough to be worth a federal agent's time, but not so ironclad that they'd ever be asked to testify. "The key is you got to know what the point of interest is in a given office today," he said.

The prosecutor who put the pair in prison, Buddy Parker, says he understands the pressures that made the information so valuable. "The only way to avoid a long sentence was to cut a cooperation deal. People without information, they're screwed," he said. "The guy who was the greatest criminal had the greatest likelihood of getting a low sentence."

Fierer got a two-and-a-half-year sentence. But he went home early after he gave agents information about another case.

Following the information, and the money

Watkins' information is still reverberating through one drug case.

In early 2008, an Atlanta jail inmate facing mortgage fraud charges approached FBI agents with information about a drug trafficker who was dealing in tractor-trailer loads of marijuana and cocaine. Leon Lumsden was by then practiced at trying to use information to win a deal. At his sentencing hearing that July, so many federal agents showed up on his behalf that the judge gave him an even bigger sentence reduction than prosecutors had sought.

The prosecutor on Lumsden's case, Gale McKenzie, had warned state and federal officers that his "credibility was nil." Still, she wrote in a September, 2008 e-mail, "many from state and federal law enforcement debriefed him and reported receiving verified information of value as well as making arrests based on his cooperation."

But the information about the drug dealer panned out. Marlon Burton — "Bird" on the street — lived in a country club south of Atlanta and traveled in a Mercedes; he had a direct connection to a Mexican cartel, according to court records.

What was less clear was how Lumsden — a white-collar crook — knew about him. During a phone interview this month, Watkins said he provided the information about Burton to Lumsden, and that he was compensated for it.

Court records show he had previously offered the same facts to federal investigators.

Lumsden insisted that the information he got from Watkins was worthless. "I didn't benefit from all the garbage he gave me," he said during a brief phone call from a Georgia prison. "Everything he gave me was straight BS."

A reliable source, and more arrests

Still, in November of 2008, the FBI used Lumsden's information to ask a federal judge to let agents wiretap the trafficker's cellphone. He was an important part of the case because the agents' other informant hadn't done business with Burton in years, meaning a judge might think it was too stale to justify a wiretap. The agent who signed the wiretap application, Nikki Badolato, told the judge that Lumsden was "reliable."

Badolato later testified that she didn't know that Lumsden had been buying information because his name was misspelled in an FBI database.

The FBI got its wiretap. Agents arrested Burton the next year.

Burton in turn informed on the other members of his organization. In return, prosecutors chopped a decade off his prison sentence, a bargain the judge called "more than generous." One of the people Burton implicated was the owner of a Lithonia, Ga., machine shop where he said he would park, and sometimes unload, truckloads of marijuana and cocaine.

Agents arrested the owner, Ivey Grant, in the drive-through line of a Sonic Drive-In. It was the first time Grant, 61, had been charged with a crime, and when FBI agents booked him they found his hands were so scoured by years of labor that his fingerprints had worn away.

Grant is serving nine years in federal prison.

He insists he didn't know what was in Burton's trucks; to him, they were just like any of the other big rigs and dump trucks that rent space in the shop's dusty parking lot. Now he's asking a federal appeals court in Atlanta to overturn his conviction, saying that the judge who approved the wiretap that ensnared him should have been told about the shaky informants behind it.

Sitting in a cinder-block prison office in Atlanta's federal prison last month, Grant sounded more confused than angry about how he ended up facing almost a decade in custody. "I don't think it's right for a convicted felon to get up on the stand in front of honest citizens and convict other people," he said.

But with seven years to go, he sees the appeal.

"If someone says you can go home today if you say that box is blue," he said, stabbing a thick finger at a big, white cardboard box in the corner of the office and grinning, "then that box is blue."

PART 1 of 2

Episode 1

Near Escape — Hold up — Almost Slipped through the Crack

It all began October 1995 in Atlanta, Georgia after months of committing numerous armed robberies on a string of grocery stores, restaurants, shops and Atlanta based drug dealers to support a crack cocaine addiction. I was arrested and taken into custody by the Atlanta Police Department only minutes after a robbery attempt and shootout with a local drug dealer in the Pittsburgh Community (Pitt) area within the city limits of Atlanta, Georgia.

Once in custody, I was taken to the Robbery Division of the Atlanta Police Department Precinct in downtown Atlanta where I was introduced to the robbery detectives that were overseeing the warrant for my arrest. I was then interviewed and formally charged with armed robbery and shortly thereafter taken to and booked into the Atlanta Pretrial Detention Center (APDC) in downtown Atlanta, Georgia.

I can't even describe the way I felt going to my first court appearance. It all happened so very fast, which was within twenty-four hours after my arrest and was held in the Atlanta Municipal Court System. I braced for all the freakin' charges I was about to face, then I learned that I was only being charged with one count of armed robbery. WTF?!! I should have been charged with double digit counts of armed robbery. You learn quickly that there is no immediate bond set, if any, within the Atlanta Municipal Court System for a charge of armed robbery. Therefore, the Atlanta Police Detectives (APDs) handling my case knew I wasn't going anywhere anytime soon and were content with me being held on one count of armed robbery. When the court called my name and read the case against me aloud, the city solicitor asked the court for a two-week continuance, which, to no one's surprise, was granted.

Shortly, after my brief court appearance, I met with the APDs that were assigned to my case and learned the reason for me being charged with and held on only one count of armed robbery and the reason for the two-week continuance. The Feds were in the process of picking up my case and bringing more charges against me on a federal level. Holy shit, was I scared! For the next two weeks, I sat nervously at APDC awaiting my next court date and the transfer of custody. When my next court date did come around and the court called my name and read the case against me, surprisingly, there were no Federal Law Enforcement Agents (FLEA) or anyone from the Atlanta Police Department there to respond to the court's call or to even prosecute the case against me. That left the court no choice but to dismiss the charge and case against me.

I repeatedly screamed in my head realizing the weight that had been lifted from my shoulders. Just when the day seemed to be going my way, things quickly changed. Immediately after the judge dismissed the charge and case against me due to lack of prosecution, the city solicitor stood and informed the court that I had a Fulton County probation violation "Hold" on me from a previous robbery case, and therefore,

I had to be transferred to the Fulton County Jail to address the probation violation issue before I could be released.

Hours after my first court appearance, I once again met with the APDs assigned to my case. I learned the reason for the detectives' and agents' absence from my court appearance. When en route to my second court appearance, APDs assigned to my case, and federal agents that later took over my case, were responding to an active armed bank robbery occurring in the West End Area of Atlanta, which is about a five-minute drive from the Atlanta Municipal Court. The APDs assigned to my case stated that while en route to the bank robbery, they called the Atlanta Solicitor's Office and informed someone there of their situation and asked that that person not only inform the court of their situation, but also requested that the court either delay calling my case until they could get there or reschedule my court case for a later date.

Somehow there was a mix-up and that person from the solicitor's office never relayed the APD's message to the court. During that meeting with the APDs assigned to my case, they joked with me about how I almost slipped through the cracks in the Atlanta judiciary system. Had it not been for that damn "Hold" on me for probation violation, I would have escaped custody that day even if it was only temporary.

Several days after my second Municipal Court appearance, I was transferred from the APDC in downtown Atlanta to the Fulton County Jail to face a Probation Revocation hearing. That was of no importance to me compared to the Federal Charges that I would soon be facing. While being housed inside of the Fulton County Jail awaiting my Probation Revocation hearing, the necessary paperwork and transfer of custody was completed resulting in a Federal "Hold" being placed on me. While housed at the Fulton County Jail, the Federal "Hold" that was placed on me signified that once the matter concerning the unimportant Probation Revocation was completed, I would then be handed over to the Feds to face unknown Federal Charges.

After several weeks of being housed at the Fulton County Jail, I was finally taken downstairs to a courtroom at the jail to face the judge presiding over my Probation Revocation hearing. Once the hearing started, I quickly informed the judge of the Federal "Hold" on me and stated to the judge that the little amount of probation time that I had left which he could revoke, was of no significance compared to the pending federal charges that awaited me.

After learning of those details, the judge postponed my probation hearing to confer with the Atlanta US Attorney's Office (Atl-USAO) regarding the alleged pending federal charges against me. After verifying the pending federal charges against me, the judge presiding over my Probation Revocation hearing immediately dismissed the remaining amount of probation time that I had left to serve and ordered that I be handed over to the custody of the US Marshal Services (USMS).

According to the United States Marshal Website, "The United States Marshals Service (USMS) is a federal law enforcement agency within the U.S. Department of Justice (28 U.S.C. § 561). It is one of the oldest U.S. federal law enforcement agencies and was created by the Judiciary Act of 1789 during the presidency of George Washington as the 'Office of the United States Marshal.' The USMS, as it stands today, was established in 1969 to provide guidance and assistance to marshals throughout the federal judicial districts. USMS is an agency of the United States executive branch reporting to the United States Attorney General, but they serve as the enforcement arm of the United States federal courts to ensure the effective operation of the judiciary and integrity of the constitution." Twisted, but their motto is "Justice, Integrity, Service". In this book, that motto will seem a bit challenged.

The Marshal's website, usmarshals.gov, also tells us that, "they have approximately 100 marshals and 4000 deputy marshals and criminal investigators as sworn members. The Marshals Service is the primary agency for fugitive operations, the protection of officers of the federal judiciary, the management of criminal assets, the operation of the United States Federal Witness Protection Program and the Justice Prisoner and Alien Transportation System, the execution of federal arrest warrants, and the protection of senior government officials through the Office of Protective Operations."

Within 72 hours after the probation judge ordered that I be handed over to the USMS, I was transferred via USMS from the Fulton County Jail to the Federal Courthouse in downtown Atlanta, Georgia. I was taken to the US Marshal's holding and intake area to be in-processed, fingerprinted and photographed. I was then placed in of one of the US Marshal's cells in the holding and intake area to await my first court appearance. When the charges against me were read audibly, the judge appointed a Federal Defender as my attorney, and I was denied bond once again, which was of no surprise to me. In the years to come, I would learn and realize that it is nearly impossible for a black defendant with an arrest record to get a bond within the Atlanta Federal Court System, 11th circuit.

At the conclusion of my first court appearance, I was returned to the US Marshal's holding cell that I previously occupied to await being transported via USMS to the old APDC, which, at the time, had been converted into a Federal Holding Facility. The old APDC is now some type of homeless shelter and is right next door to the current APDC in downtown Atlanta, where I was previously held on one count of armed robbery at the beginning of my incarceration.

Upon arriving at the old APDC, I was placed in a general population housing unit consisting of over twenty more federal defendants, whom I would be housed with for several months to come. Even though the majority of the occupants in the housing unit were Black, I could at least say that the Feds didn't discriminate. Among the many Black defendants being housed in the same unit as me, there were at least three Caucasian and several Mexican defendants housed there as well. Later, I found that there were, in fact, several housing units filled to capacity with only Black defendants.

After days of being housed at the old APDC, I finally met with my court appointed Federal Defender, Paul Kish, who would be representing me throughout the ordeal. Paul Kish, who is Caucasian, now has his own law firm and is one of the most sought-after Attorneys in the city of Atlanta. The first of many meetings to come with Mr. Kish took place in a designated Attorney Room on the first floor of the old APDC several floors beneath my housing unit at the time. I was skeptical about the legal representation that I would be receiving from him, being that the Federal Defender Program for which he worked for was actually being funded by the same government that was prosecuting me.

After a formal introduction, Mr. Kish and I got down to business. The first matter of business was the twenty-plus count indictment that outlined the charges against me. Upon review of my twenty plus count indictment, I realized that instead of numerous counts of armed robbery, the government was charging me with numerous counts of interfering with Interstate Commerce, which I had no understanding of until Mr. Kish explained the charge to me. Interfering with Interstate Commerce is just fancy wording used by the government for the crime of robbery/theft committed against the type of businesses that I was robbing to support my crack cocaine addiction. Besides the numerous counts of Interfering with Interstate Commerce, I was also charged with a 924(c) gun charge, which is referred to by legislated law as: governing and brandishing of a firearm in the commission of a crime. After Mr. Kish and I reviewed the charges against me and reviewed the sentencing guidelines. We both came to the same conclusion; I was facing a lot of prison time. However, the amount of prison time that I was facing on the Federal level was of no comparison to the amount of prison time that I would have been facing had my crimes of armed robbery remained on the state indictment. "God, please send me back to state jurisdiction," is all I was crying to myself. I was honestly afraid and disappointed that my life was about to waste away behind bars.

Over the next few months, Mr. Kish and I met on several occasions to discuss court motions that he had filed with the court on my behalf, other avenues of defense and to discuss the possibility of taking my case to trial. It was during that same time (between December 1995 and February 1996) in which the government submitted to my attorney the "only" plea agreement that would be offered in my case. The plea agreement that the government submitted to my attorney sought to resolve my Federal Court case (Fed-case) with a prison sentence of 188 months (15 and 1/2 years), which I rejected. Hell no! My reason for rejecting the government's submitted plea agreement is because, by that time, my attorney had convinced me that he could beat some, if not all, of the interfering with Interstate Commerce charges at trial. From that point on, Mr. Kish and I prepared for what would be a federal bench trial, not a federal jury trial.

Exhibit A–2

Robert A. Deyton Detention Facility
Revised 11/28/08

Notice of Detention / Protective Custody Placement / Waiver Form

GEO The GEO Group, Inc.

Date:	Shift:
Friday, December 14, 2012	**1st Shift 0600-1400 Hours**

Shift Supervisor: (Print Name)	Shift Supervisor Signature
SGT Palmer	

A.

Detainee Name:	**WATKINS, MARCUS**
Detainee U.S.M.S. Number	**46440019**
Date of Segregation / Placement	**Friday, December 14, 2012**
Time of Segregation / Placement	**1100 Hours**
Previous Housing Unit Assignment	**104B**
New Housing Unit Assignment:	**203B**
Segregation Status:	

If the detainee was placed into segregation status for Pre-Hearing Detention or a Disciplinary violation, Please list the Detainee Conduct Code Violation(s):

	Voluntary Protective Custody
	Release from Protective Custody
X	Involuntary Protective Custody
	Placement into the Detainee General Pop.
	Administrative Segregation
	Custody Level
	Disciplinary
	Pre-seg Detention
	Sentence Structure
	Seperation Order
	Suicide Watch
	Violent Behavior

1. **N/A**   3. **N/A**

2. **N/A**   4. **N/A.**

B.

Detainee _____ **WATKINS, MARCUS** _____

has been placed onto _____ **Involuntary Protective Custody** _____ Segregation Status by the authority

of _____ **SGT Palmer** _____ For: **Involuntary Protective Custody**

Detainee Signature: _____   Date: _____ **12/14/12**

SGT J. Palmer   Staff Member Signature:
Staff Member Print:

2nd Staff Member Print: 2nd Staff Member Signature:
(If detainee refuses to sign).   (If detainee refuses to sign).

Page (1) of (2)

Note: This document must be completed upon segregation placement or release.

Robert A. Deyton Detention Facility

Revised 11/28/08

Notice of Detention / Protective Custody Placement / Waiver Form

GEO
The GEO Group, Inc.

C. Detainee ___**WATKINS, MARCUS**___ has received a copy of his /
her property inventory.

Detainee Signature: _____   Date: ___**12/14/12**___

___**SGT J.Palmer**___   _____
Staff Member Print: Staff Member Signature:

_____   _____
2nd Staff Member Print: 2nd Staff Member Signature:
(If detainee refuses to sign).   (If detainee refuses to sign).

D. I, Detainee ___**N/A**___ *do / do not* request (circle one) protective
Custody Status. I *do / do not* (circle one) fear for my safety. I *do / do not* (circle one) wish to be placed
into the detainee General Population. I will comply with an accept all of the Institutional rules of the Robert
A. Deyton Detention Facility. I have no animosity towards or have an intention(s) or motives to do harm
to or know of any other detainee that wishes to do harm to myself.

Detainee ___**WATKINS, MARCUS**___ is being placed onto Involuntary Protective
Custody Status due to the best interest of the detainee and the Robert A. Deyton Detention Facility.

Reason / Comment: _____**Per directive of the Wardon**_____
_____
_____
_____

Detainee Signature: _____   Date: ___**12/14/12**___

___**SGT J. Palmer**___   Date: 12/14/12   _____
Staff Member Print: Staff Member Signature:

_____   Date: _____   _____
2nd Staff/ Witness Print: 2nd Staff Witness Signature:
(Mandatory whether detainee refuses or signs).   (Mandatory whether detainee refuses or signs).

Page (2) of (2)

Note: This document must be completed upon segregation placement or release.

Episode II

Federal Invites of a Pittsburg Snitch vs. Pittsburg Gangsters

March 25, 1996 was the start of my bench trial in the Honorable Judge Willis B. Hunt, Jr.'s federal courtroom in Atlanta, Georgia. A bench trial is where all the evidence and witnesses are presented to the judge presiding over the case, and your guilt or innocence is left to the judge to determine.

Prior to the start of my bench trial, I entered a no-lo-contendere plea to the 924(c) gun charge, essentially a guilty plea with no contest to the charge, effectively resulting in a conviction even before the start of my trial. Whereas Mr. Kish and I both agreed that I could not beat the 924(c) gun charge, we sought only to fight the Interfering with Interstate Commerce charges. My trial only lasted a few days, and the end result supported that Mr. Kish had done exactly what he said he could do. He beat some of the Interfering with Interstate Commerce charges.

From the over twenty counts of Interfering with Interstate Commerce, Judge Hunt found me guilty of only six counts. On July 2, 1996, I was brought back to Federal Court to be sentenced for the six counts of Interfering with Interstate Commerce that Judge Hunt found me guilty of committing, for which I received a sentence of 151 months (12 years 7 months). For the 924(c) gun charge that I entered no-contest to, I received a 60-month prison sentence. When it was all said and done, I had received 211 months (17 years 7 months) prison sentence. My dumb ass should have taken the government's initial plea agreement (never listen to jailhouse lawyers nor challenge the Feds with only pride filling the traps of your lungs). Mr. Kish filed an appeal on my behalf as he felt that he could beat at least four of the remaining six counts of Interfering with Interstate Commerce charges in which I was convicted of and sentenced.

After sentencing, I was transported via USMS to the United States Penitentiary (USP), Atlanta, Georgia to await being designated. So allow me to give you a perspective on United States Penitentiaries in both Atlanta and Leavenworth as I will write about both in this book:

United States Penitentiary, Atlanta (USP Atlanta)

The United States Penitentiary, Atlanta (USP Atlanta) is a maximum-security United States federal prison for male inmates in Atlanta, Georgia. The facility also has a detention center for pretrial and holdover inmates, and a satellite prison camp for minimum-security male inmates. In the 1980s, USP Atlanta was used as a detention center for Cuban refugees from the Mariel Boatlift who were ineligible for release into American society. USP Atlanta is currently one of several facilities, including the Federal Transfer Center, Oklahoma City, that are used to house prisoners who are being transferred between prisons. As of 2006, the prison was housing three to five in-transit prisoners in each approximately 8'x7', 56-square-foot (5.2 m^2) isolation cell for up to eight weeks at a time.

United States Penitentiary, USP Leavenworth

The United States Penitentiary, Leavenworth (USP Leavenworth) is a medium security U.S. penitentiary with an adjacent minimum security satellite camp in northeast Kansas. It is operated by the Federal Bureau of Prisons (FBP), a division of the United States Department of Justice. It also includes a satellite Federal Prison Camp (FPC) for minimum-security male offenders.

The prison population is around 1900 of which a third of that is in prison camp. USP Leavenworth, a civilian facility, is located in Leavenworth, Kansas, 25 miles northwest of Kansas City, Kansas, It is the oldest of three major prisons built on federal land in Leavenworth County, Kansas. It is separate from, but often confused with, the non-civilian facility, United States Disciplinary Barracks (USDB), a military facility located on the adjacent Fort Leavenworth Army base located 4 miles north of the USP. The USDB is the sole maximum-security penal facility for the entire United States Military. Prisoners from the original USDB were used to build the civilian penitentiary. In addition, the military's medium-security Midwest Joint Regional Correctional Facility (JRCF), located southwest of the new USDB, opened in 2010. The USDB and JRCF operate independently from USP Leavenworth.

USP Leavenworth was the largest maximum-security federal prison in the United States from 1903 to 2005. However, it was downgraded to a medium-security facility.

Photo from Bureau of Prisons USP Leavenworth website: www.bop.gov

Arriving at the Federal Prison in Atlanta, I was processed (fingerprinted and photographed) and then taken to the DCU-1 Low Security and Pretrial Housing Unit, where I spent the next four and a half weeks. I was then designated to USP Leavenworth located in Leavenworth, Kansas which automatically raised my security level to "High." Once my security level was raised, I could no longer be housed in the DCU-1 Low Security and Pretrial Housing Unit and, therefore, was moved to the DCU-2 Medium/High Security Housing Unit, which is one floor above the DCU-1. A week after being designated and moved to DCU-2, I was flown via Federal Bureau of Prisons (FBP) aircraft to USP Leavenworth where I spent about two weeks.

Two weeks into my stay at USP Leavenworth, I was informed that I would be going out to court the following morning on a "writ," and I was instructed to "pack it up," which I did gladly. When told that I was headed back to court, I could only assume that the appeal process had already taken its course. Little did I know, that was not the case. The next morning, I was flown via FBP aircraft back to Atlanta, Georgia and returned to USP Atlanta. Once back at USP Atlanta and after going through the entire intake procedure again, I was placed back into the DCU-2 Housing Unit where I spent the next two and a half years!

It was September 1996 and once back at USP Atlanta's DCU-2 Housing Unit, I crossed the path of numerous guys from Atlanta, some that I knew personally, whereas others I knew by face or distant association. Although arrested on federal drug charges, most of them were very successful, well connected, and well-respected drug dealers from the inner-city — metro Atlanta and Decatur areas. I mean, they were moving and supplying large quantities of cocaine, tens to hundreds of kilos, throughout the city of Atlanta and surrounding areas during the late 1980's and early 1990's. One in particular, T-

Rock, was from my neighborhood, the Pitt community. He was approximately five years older than me, and he's actually one of the hustlers that I and many other guys around my age looked up to. For several days I'd see T-Rock and the same group of drug dealers sitting around huddled up, basically communicating with only those in their inner circle. T-Rock and I kicked it with each other daily, even though I wasn't privileged to be a part of that circle.

Two days later, USMS took me to the Federal Courthouse in downtown Atlanta to attend to matters that I assumed were related to the existing appeal. So now I went through the intake process and waited in a holding cell to be called out. Thankfully, that holding cell experience was short lived, and when called out, I was escorted by the Deputy US Marshal to an attorney booth to meet with my attorney, Mr. Kish. He wasted no time informing me that I was not brought back from USP Leavenworth to attend to any matters pertaining to my appeal. Rather, I was brought back at the request of FLEAs and Atl-USAO. He then stated that the appeal that we had filed was not a sure thing, but the deal that those individuals were going to offer to me was a guarantee, and, therefore, I should really consider accepting the deal that was about to be offered. That was that.

Upon Arriving back at the US Marshal's intake and holding area, I was then placed in the custody of two FLEAs unknown to me. Once in custody of those FLEAs, I was taken to an office within the Atl-USAO where the arranged meeting took place. In attendance were the two FLEA escorts, an Atl-USAO officer, Mr. Kish and I. After all the introductions were out of the way, the two FLEAs that I now knew as members of the High Intensity Drug Trafficking Area (HIDTA) Task Force (TF) and the Atl-USAO representative got right down to business. So let's take a look at the role of HIDTA.

According to the DEA's, www.dea.gov, website:

The High Intensity Drug Trafficking Areas (HIDTA) program, created by Congress with the Anti-Drug Abuse Act of 1988, provides assistance to Federal, state, local, and tribal law enforcement agencies operating in areas determined to be critical drug-trafficking regions of the United States. This grant program is administered by the Office of National Drug Control Policy (ONDCP). There are currently 28 HIDTAs, which include approximately 18 percent of all counties in the United States and 66 percent of the U.S. population. HIDTA-designated counties are located in 49 states, as well as in Puerto Rico, the U.S. Virgin Islands, and the District of Columbia. The DEA plays a very active role and has nearly 600 authorized special agent positions dedicated to the program. At the local level, the HIDTAs are directed and guided by Executive Boards composed of an equal number of regional Federal and non-Federal (state, local, and tribal) law enforcement leaders.

The purpose of the HIDTA program is to reduce drug trafficking and production in the United States by:

Facilitating cooperation among Federal, state, local, and tribal law enforcement agencies to share information and implement coordinated enforcement activities;

Enhancing law enforcement intelligence sharing among Federal, state, local, and tribal law enforcement agencies;

Providing reliable law enforcement intelligence to law enforcement agencies to facilitate the design of effective enforcement strategies and operations; and

Supporting coordinated law enforcement strategies that make the most of available resources to reduce the supply of illegal drugs in designated areas of the United States and in the Nation as a whole.

So first off, they started by explaining why I was brought back to Atlanta from USP Leavenworth, what they wanted from me, and what it was that they were offering me. In a matter of minutes, it became very clear to me that they wanted me to become a Confidential Informant for the government — A SNITCH! It was also at that time I learned that they wanted me to rat on a very dangerous and violent group of guys from my own neighborhood known as the "Pittsburgh Gangsters" aka PBG. The members of PBG were responsible for several murders, numerous shootings, beatings, and distribution of large quantities of crack cocaine in and around the Pitt area.

In the course of explaining what it was that they wanted from me and what it was that they were offering me, I also learned the reason why they had chosen me, of all people, to "snitch" on the members of the PBG. Somehow, they were privy to the fact that I was at odds with a high-ranking member of the group stemming from a 1993 incident. In December 1993, I robbed one of the PBG crack cocaine distribution locations, an apartment belonging to the crew's high-ranking member. Several days after committing that robbery, I was involved in a shootout with him, but also that of numerous lower ranking PBG members as well, spurring the involvement of the Atlanta Police Department, resulting in my arrest.

After telling me who it was that they wanted me to snitch on, the representative from the Atl-USAO then explained to me that at the conclusion of my cooperation, their office would file a Rule 35 Sentence Reduction Motion with the court on my behalf. It was during this particular meeting that I not only learned that a Rule 35 is a Sentence Reduction Motion filed by the government for cooperation that is rendered to the government within one year after being sentenced, but that a 5k1.1 is a sentence reduction motion that is filed by the government for cooperation that is rendered to the government prior to being sentenced.

At the conclusion of that meeting, I was told that I would be given a week to make my decision on whether I would accept the deal that had just been offered. I was then escorted from the Atl-USAO by the same FLEAs back to the US Marshal's intake and holding area. Once back at the US Marshal's intake and holding area, I was placed back in the custody of the US Marshals, and you know the drill from here: holding cell for however long, hurry up and wait to be transported back to USP Atlanta.

Upon arriving back at the Federal Prison in Atlanta (USP Atlanta), I had to endure the normal procedure of being strip-searched by FBP corrections officers before being taken back to the DCU-2 Housing Unit. Once back inside of the DCU-2 Housing Unit, the first thing that I did was go looking for my homeboy, T-Rock, to tell him how the Atl-USAO and FLEAs just tried my gangsta. "Street loyalty over everything" was my motto! Death before dishonor! After catching him up on what transpired that day at court, I was shocked when T-Rock informed me that he and all of the Atlanta drug dealers that he was seen sitting and huddled up with have all been cooperating, snitching for the government on a variety of individuals and suspect activity in hopes of receiving a 5k1.1 or Rule 35 Sentence Reduction. T-Rock then stated profoundly, "Those who pray stay, but those who talk walk." No joke! A very true statement, I came to learn.

At that very moment, I decided to break my loyalty to the street code and spread my wings like an Atlanta Hawk or Falcon. I called my attorney first thing the next morning to let him know that I would be accepting the deal I was offered. Promptly, Mr. Kish contacted the representative from the Atl-USAO to let her know everything was a go. Oddly, several minutes after informing my attorney, there was an assault on a female staff member within one of the two DCU housing units. That resulted in both of the DCU

Housing Units being completely locked down on a twenty-three and one lock-down status for an extended period. Can you count to 10.......YEARS, that is? Ten years! A 23/1 lock-down status is where the inmates are locked down in their cells for twenty-three straight hours a day and allowed one hour per day, Monday-Friday, to shower, use the telephones, and utilize one of the two recreation cages within the one hour time frame. Fucked up and far more mentally challenging than one could ever imagine.

After several weeks of being confined to my cell on twenty-three and one lock down housing status, I was assigned to a dorm orderly detail which allowed me to roam freely in the DCU-2 Housing Unit. Once out of my cell and able to roam around the dormitory freely, I learned that during the first few days of that lock-down status, T-Rock had been transferred back to the Federal Prison that he was serving his time at. He too was back in Atlanta on a "writ" for the purpose of snitching. I didn't see or speak to T-Rock again until the summer of 2002 at which time he and I were both free, back in the hood.

Episode III

The "Blue" Trap

It was late September 1996, and I had recently become a DCU-2 dorm orderly. Several days passed, and I realized that all of the other dorm orderlies were either from the city of Atlanta or caught their Federal Case in Atlanta. There were seven of them. They all were back in Atlanta on a "writ" and were — yep, you guessed it — all snitching! They were shamelessly cooperating with the government in hopes of receiving a 5k1.1 or Rule 35 Sentence Reduction. Like I said, shamelessly; several of them boldly had rhymes to complement the snitching that they were doing. For instance, I heard one guy say:

> *"You could call me a rat, a bitch, and a snitch, but just don't call me collect, because I'm go'n be gone, I'm going home."*

Another guy had actually changed the lyrics of an old R & B song called Magic Man to lyrics that complemented his snitching. The original lyrics to the song say:

> *"I'll pull a rabbit out of a hat, disappear and return just like that. Cause baby I'm your magic man, yes, I am. Tricks with cards are easy to do. But tricks with hearts will cast a spell on you. Cause baby I'm your magic man, yes I am,"*

This guy had changed the lyrics to say:

> *"I'll pull a rabbit out of a hat, go to Federal Prison and come home just like that. Cause baby I'm your magic man, yes, I am. Tricks with cards are easy to do. But this 5k1.1/Rule 35 is going to cast a spell on you. Cause baby I'm your magic man, yes I am."*

Hmm, lmao! I bet you got a laugh outta that too.

During that time, all of the DCU-2 dorm orderlies, including myself, were hired by the counselor assigned to the DCU-2 Housing Unit, a black female by the name of Marquita Grayer. After several weeks of being a dorm orderly, Mrs. Grayer promoted me to the head orderly position. Several weeks after being promoted to the head orderly position, I began a romantic and sexual relationship with Mrs. Grayer that would last until the winter months of 1998. During our relationship, we engaged in sexual activity on numerous occasions in a storage room and an office one floor below the DCU-2 Housing Unit.

It is also during the course of me being a dorm orderly that I came in contact with an inmate by the name of Gregory Harris, originally from Detroit, Michigan, but caught his Federal case in Atlanta, Georgia. And yes, he too was snitching on a variety of individuals and situations. He was snitching at the time on a level I had yet to reach and is also named in the December 14, 2012 USA Today newspaper article. Within a matter of days after becoming a dorm orderly, I started my life of snitching by attending what would be the first of many debriefings to come. While housed at the Federal Prison in Atlanta, all of my debriefings between the time of September 1996 and October 1998 were conducted inside of an office or conference room located in the Atl-USAO. Prior to the beginning of my first debriefing my attorney had me sign a waiver waiving my appeal. Being that I was now cooperating with the government, I could no longer appeal my conviction, nor did I need to.

Those in attendance at my first debriefing consisted of individuals from FLEAs, HIDTA TF and the representative from the Atl-USAO, who had previously presented the cooperation deal to me. My first debriefing started off by the HIDTA TF Agents showing me a photo book consisting of numerous up-close photos of members of the PBG, and also photos of every hustler and criminal, male and female from the Pittsburgh community. I was then asked to identify the individuals in each photo by name and to point out the members of the PBG. After successfully completing that task, it became obvious to me that those agents were only testing me to see if I was going to be honest with them. They already knew all or most of the answers to the questions they asked.

It was during my second debriefing pertaining to the notorious members of the PBG that I would learn from the HIDTA TF Agents and members of the USAO in attendance that a heavyweight drug dealer from the Pittsburgh community (former Pittsburgh Civic League Apartments) named Russell Liverpool a.k.a 'Cat' had recently been arrested and wasted no time informing the same HIDTA TF Agents and the USAO that he was willing to provide in depth intel on anyone he knew with street affiliation, especially members of the PBG he was associated with in hopes of receiving a 5K1.1 Sentencing Reduction. He was talking so much that they had to duct tape his mouth while he slept. I, on the other hand, was 10 toes in like a Marine on the Afghanistan battlefield. My mission was to gain beneficial intel, snitch, and successfully receive a reward from the USAO.

In 1996, Russell Liverpool a.k.a 'Cat' and co-conspirators were arrested on Federal drug charges (case no: 1:96-CR-455) and being that Russell Liverpool was supplying the members of the PBG with large quantities of drugs, paying members of the street organization for protection, and paying the members to commit violent crimes on his behalf which he later confessed to for the sole purpose of not jeopardizing his sentencing reduction. At one point the HIDTA TF Agents and members of the Atl-USAP thought Russell Liverpool was actually the leader of the Pittsburgh Gangsters, only to discover differently.

Due to the severity of Russell Liverpool's Federal drug charges, he was initially facing significantly more federal time than the 17 years and 7 months that I received from my bench trial. However, as a result of his substantial cooperation to help secure indictments and convictions on several members of the PBG organization and other individuals involved in heavy criminal activity, Mr. Liverpool received a significant sentence reduction which allowed him to be released from Federal prison in 2002 almost beating me home even though he got arrested after my 1995 arrest.

Over the course of the next two years (1996-1998), I engaged in numerous debriefings solely pertaining to the PBG. This put me in contact with several other members of the Atl-USAO. Those debriefings eventually led to me appearing and providing testimony before the Grand Jury. Days prior, I was subjected to several prep sessions conducted by Officer 'X' of the Atl-USAO. During those prep sessions, Officer 'X' was extremely focused on telling me what to say, diligently providing me with information that she wanted and needed me to testify in the presence of the Grand Jury. Within a few days, Officer 'X' sought to get a Federal Indictment listing multiple charges against members of the PBG.

Member 'X' of the Atl-USAO was so concerned with preparing me to convey specific information to the assembled grand jury that it seemingly never once crossed her mind to become familiar with the Federal charges that I had been convicted of. I acknowledge this because during my testimony, she assumed that I had been convicted on Federal Drug Charges in err, only to shockingly discover, in the presence of the assembled grand jury, the federal charges that I had actually been convicted of. The USAO was so focused on perfecting a testimony of lies that the simple truth shined a light upon their incompetence.

To the surprise of all the members of the Atl-USAO and FLEAs involved in the relentless effort to bring Federal charges against the members of the PBG, the True Bill sought, in truth, was a "No Bill" Indictment returned in court against the members of the Pittsburgh Gangsters — not today! Choked! Sorry Charlie! They were all stunned that a "True Bill" Indictment was not returned with the substantial testimony provided. Personally, it didn't matter at all to me one way or another whether a True Bill indictment was returned. The end result would be the same for me, no matter what. The government (Atl-USAO) would still have to pay me in the form of a Rule 35 Sentence Reduction for my newly profound services, snitching. In many ways I was actually happy I didn't have to testify against any of the members because my selfishness could have brought harm to members of my family as a way of getting me to recant my testimony, and my street cred was still considered solid. The bottom line was that the individuals I grew up with and who considered me a true friend never knew I betrayed them for my own benefit. Whether or not I was honestly trying to get back to the street to smoke some crack instead of being with my family and rectifying my life, all that mattered was my services were for sale. My new hustle was snitching, and I was definitely going to benefit.

Years after the HIDTA TF Agents' and members of the Atl-USAO's failed attempt to secure a Federal indictment against the members of the Pittsburgh Gangsters, they used tainted evidence and falsified information to successfully obtain a Federal indictment on Federal drug charges against the PBG members Billy Giles and Gregory Buchanan a.k.a "Blue" (case no: 1:99-CR-289), whom just so happen to be blood relatives, first cousins. Two wrongs shouldn't suffer and every man for himself was seemingly how Gregory Buchanan viewed the entire situation, which undoubtedly caused him to make a closed-door deal with the USAO.

Seeking to return back to the streets by any means necessary, while severing the bond of family and loyalty, G. Buchanan helped the USAO secure a conviction against his co-defendant Billy Giles (cousin), by openly testifying information he knew the HIDTA TF Agents and the Atl-USAO provided for him to say was fraudulent. As for the writing of this book, Billy Giles has served 20 years of his Federal prison sentence and his cousin Gregory Buchanan remained a free man for a time period exceeding 10 years. The game is what it is.

You may be wondering how I was knowledgeable of the plot against defendant Billy Giles or can actually acknowledge the testimony against him contained fraudulent information the HIDTA TF Agents and USAO provided with injustice intended. Honestly, it's not just because of the things that were openly shared with me by certain HIDTA TF Agents and USAO individuals during a few meetings as the government built their criminal case. I stand by my words because at the time of that government plot against defendant Billy Giles, those same HIDTA TF Agents and select members of the USAO made it possible for defendant Billy Giles, his cousin Gregory Buchanan, and me to be housed within the same facility at the APDC in downtown Atlanta, Georgia. The USAO also made arrangements with the officials at the facility to have me housed within the same inmate dormitory with defendant Billy Giles so that I could keep them informed of any event Giles and his attorney became knowledgeable of concerning their plot or the fraudulent information their government witness, Gregory Buchanan, would be testifying to against his cousin (Billy Giles) which they provided. My cooperation was once again a beneficial service that resulted in a personal gain solely for myself. At this particular time of my incarceration, I was back in Atlanta on my second 'writ' awaiting my Rule 35 Sentence Reduction hearing. I was working!

The reasoning behind the plot against and determination to arrest and convict defendant Billy Giles was nothing less than karma. HIDTA TF Agents and members of the USAO would openly joke during our meetings. In 1995, Billy Giles committed a murder in broad daylight before numerous witnesses within the city of Atlanta, and he was later apprehended by the Atlanta Police Department but was later acquitted at trial thanks to witness tampering and witness intimidation by outside members of his PBG crew. It just so happened that at the particular time of that 1995 murder, members of the Atlanta Police Department were also members of the HIDTA Task Force and they didn't like the fact he used fear tactics to dissuade the witness in testifying and get acquitted.

Episode IV

Modern Day Ziklag Moment — ZIPLAG Manna

Throughout the course of my debriefings, solely pertaining to the PBG, FLEAs and the members of the Atl-USAO in attendance also realized that I was well connected to external sources and that I could use them to obtain current sought-after information for FLEAs and USAO members I had not done business with. Because of those reasons, I came in contact with other FLEAs and Atl-USAO members that eventually led to debriefings pertaining to individuals and topics of consideration unrelated to the PBG, so they became repeat customers.

In later years, my external sources became vital in the selling of information, and the debriefings fueled by the information that I had obtained for the buyers also went towards my Rule 35 Sentence Reduction. It was after the conclusion of one of those unrelated debriefings and in the process of being prepared to be transported back to USP Atlanta that the following incident occurred. After being handcuffed and placed in ankle shackles at the US Marshal's intake and holding area, which, by the way, is now designed much differently than it was during the time of 1996-1998, I and the other five federal inmates that were being prepared to be transported were all placed against a wall within the US Marshal's intake holding area while the two transporting Deputy US Marshals went through a door leading to a hallway area to retrieve their weapons/firearms that had been secured within lock boxes located in that hallway area. While the two transporting Deputy US Marshals went to retrieve their weapons, the other five federal inmates and I were being watched and guarded by one of the older in-house Deputy US Marshals.

During that brief period of time, I observed what appeared to be a Ziploc® bag containing what was believed to be numerous single bags of crack cocaine within the US Marshal's intake and holding area simply lying on the floor. Seconds after making that observation, I made the other five federal inmates aware of what I had seen.

Not so surprisingly, one of those inmates then walked over and retrieved the Ziploc® bag, curiously drawn by the prospect of its contents. Now, I clarify for you that these events occurred while in handcuffs and ankle shackles in the presence of a Deputy US Marshal. After retrieving the Ziploc® bag containing many individual bags of suspected crack cocaine, the inmate returned to his original position on the wall beside me and the other federal inmates. He opened the Ziploc® bag and removed one of the individual packs to sample its contents, confirming that it was indeed crack cocaine to all of us and was overheard by an older Deputy US Marshal who was standing watch over us.

Hearing this, the guard walked over and took the Ziploc® bag from the inmate. So, one would think that was the end of it, right? Far from it, we were all shocked that instead of securing the Ziploc® bag of contraband, the Deputy US Marshal threw it back on the floor exactly where I first noticed it. But wait!

There's more if you haven't bought into the madness quite yet; an authentic "Ripley's Believe it or Not®" moment, he abandoned the area, albeit momentarily. I mean, maybe the old guy was just cool like that, we all guessed.

After witnessing this unbelievable, yet true and surreal act by the Deputy US Marshal, let's just call him Deputy David, we inmates extrapolated, deducing that his silent yet loud gesture was his way of indicating to us to act like we had some sense. Meaning we should covertly grab the Ziploc® bag containing the crack cocaine, just not while he was there witnessing the whole thing idiots! Deputy David had left the building! That being the case, we were free and clear to do just that. The inmate that had previously taken possession now had a modified "modern day Ziklag moment" in the making. He walked back over and retook possession of the Ziploc® bag discarded in its original resting place on the floor — acting like he had some sense or balls or whatever. Imagine that.

For this modified "modern day Ziklag moment", I will refer to this inmate as "Ziplag" from this point on. Fair enough? OK. Upon lifting or retrieval of the Ziploc® bag, inmate Ziplag took a few moments to visually inspect it, sporting a facial expression of panning for gold on "government floors" and striking it rich. Not sure why the repeat inspection — perhaps in amusement that a gift from the crack gods manifested itself in a mysterious way. For by grace, Ziplag's art of possession was granted a second chance at life — or "lift," I should say. Hesitatingly, he concealed the crystalline manna from drug heaven in his jacket's right pocket. Timing was too perfect; like clockwork, it was mere seconds after securing the rained down crack manna that Deputy David and the other transporting Deputy US Marshal returned to the scene and simply proceeded to transport us back to USP Atlanta — just like that. Where they do that at? If I was to change the title of this book to "What Really Happens Behind Prison Walls", I would truly cause your mouth to drop in disbelief and disgust, while fueling you with the desire to protest "all" sitting senators for turning a blind eye to the cruel and unusual punishment, physical and sexual abuse, but more so the refugee like living conditions, merely so the system can make money.

Once onboard the US Marshal's transporting van and en route, inmate Ziplag, profound with joy, unsealed the Ziploc® bag and started counting aloud...you heard me, rather read me — aloud! He was counting the individual bags on the inside of the Ziploc® bag that contained the crack cocaine. When he reached the count of seventy, the transporting Deputy US Marshals received a call over the van's communication system from a dispatcher somewhere within the US Marshal's intake and holding area at the Atlanta Federal Courthouse. The communication was informing them that evidentiary contraband had been removed from the intake holding area, potentially by one of us six inmates being transported back to USP Atlanta. The dispatcher then instructed the two transporting Deputy US Marshals to search us thoroughly for the missing contraband.

One would assume that inmate Ziplag in possession of the Ziploc® bag would panic after hearing that communication then at least attempt to get it off his person. You would think, right? But, shockingly, that wasn't the case. Not sure why I'm surprised at this point, but I am. We stopped at USP Atlanta, the two transporters simply escorted us up one floor to the intake area, removed our handcuffs and ankle shackles and placed the six of us into a holding cell, then they left. That's it? Yeah...that's it...end of story. The two transporting deputy US Marshals had disregarded the communications as abruptly as the older marshal discarded the contraband.

Several minutes after being placed in the holding cell, we got the scoop that an airlift and a bus full of inmates had arrived and had been processed prior to our landing. The tedious effort must have resulted in an inconvenience, oversight, or lethargic behavior by the FBP corrections guards working the intake area that day. We were eventually called out of the holding cell one by one. Each of us should've gone through the required strip-search procedure in a clothing room also located within the intake area. However, we were simply called out and issued a change of clothes prior to being shuffled into another holding cell then escorted back to our preassigned housing units. Ripley's! Unbelievable!

That's when the other four inmates and I ascertained that inmate Ziplag was still in possession of the contraband. I found out that he was at Federal Court that day attending to matters pertaining to him smuggling drugs into USP Atlanta through the visitation area of the prison prior to being re-designated from USP Atlanta to USP Leavenworth. He was housed in the Segregated Housing Unit (SHU) of USP Atlanta, also back in Atlanta on a writ, and this info would be very useful in pinpointing his whereabouts the following day.

Episode V

Greed to be Freed — Gets a Little Harry

Having returned to the DCU-2 Housing Unit on the day of the ZIPLAG discovery, I sought to consult with an inmate named Gregory Harris about the prior events of that day. At that time, he was not only an orderly like me, but a seasoned veteran at the snitching game (See Exhibit B-1). While I was head dorm orderly, I found that Gregory Harris was selling information to other inmates to be used in their favor to be granted 5k1.1 and/or Rule 35 Sentence Reductions.

At that time, FLEAs and members of the Atl-USAO had yet to certify me as a member of their inner circle, unlike Harris. Therefore, I was not privy to the selling of information and should have had no knowledge of this encouraged practice. After locating and informing inmate Gregory Harris of all the events of the day regarding the discovery of the crack cocaine, he stated to me that the knowledge of this incident would qualify as "substantial assistance", resulting in a Rule 35 Sentence Reduction for me. He then informed me that I should report the entire matter to Mrs. Grayer (DCU-2 counselor) first thing the next morning, ignorant of the fact that I was romantically and sexually involved with Mrs. Grayer. Approximately 8:00 AM the following morning, Mrs. Grayer arrived at her office within the DCU-2 Housing Unit and found me awaiting her arrival.

Once she and I entered her office, she sat at her desk. I sat in front of her and wasted no time informing her of the entire incident pertaining to the crack cocaine and its current coordinates. Within seconds of hearing all the details, Mrs. Grayer proceeded to call and report the matter to the prison's Special Investigations Services (SIS) and to the prison's on-duty supervisor. Excellent, but before I could inform Mrs. Grayer, Gregory Harris had gone behind my back and phoned the FLEA that he was cooperating with and proceeded to report everything that I had told him about ZIPLAG! Did Harris just attempt to take credit for my ZIPLAG experience, stealing the dubious dishonor right from under my nose. Mrs. Grayer came to me out of the blue later that afternoon revealing the shocker of Gregory Harris' actions and intent. Lesson learned. Guys can talk that hardcore gangster and true to the game shit all they want, but after the Gregory Harris experience, I would never again underestimate the next man's greed to be freed nor jeopardize mine.

After Mrs. Grayer reported the incident, a team of prison guards were sent to the prison's SHU where inmate Ziplag resided, and the prison guards' supervisor instructed one of them to inform Inmate Ziplag that he had an attorney's visit and that he needed to cuff up. His cellmate was also handcuffed in accordance with normal security procedure prior to any of the cell doors located in SHU being opened. After both inmates were in handcuffs and the water in the cell was turned off, escaping the cell's occupants, the cell door was opened, and the team of prison guards stormed the scene securing both inmates and proceeding to search the cell. Within a matter of minutes, the prison guards struck gold by finding individual bags of crack cocaine. But get this — both inmates had been up all night smoking the stuff, so by that time, guards only confiscated thirty plus individual packets, the residual of one hundred $10 bags originally contained in the Ziploc® bag.

If by chance you are wondering if seeing and being in the presence of all that crack cocaine had any effect on me, such as craving and/or withdrawal symptoms as a result of my prior crack cocaine addiction, wonder no more. It had a profound effect on me — it was hard, I mean really hard not to ask him to share a few, especially given I'm the one who located the treasure, crack manna, in the first place. However, knowing not only the effects that crack cocaine had on me prior to my arrest but also that I could not obtain the drug at will, deterred me from seeking to have it supplied for my personal use. The nature of my incarceration dictated my self-control.

Later that afternoon, Mrs. Grayer received a telephone call in her office from the prison's SIS, once again inquisitive of the source of the tip-off information. She responded accordingly. There seemed to be a conflict of the source, because the caller informed Mrs. Grayer that an inmate by the name of Gregory Harris was also trying to get the credit for providing that same information to a Federal Agent who had also called the prison's SIS to report the matter just minutes after Mrs. Grayer's call. That made me feel some type of way, obviously. Though I would ultimately receive the credit for reporting the incident, Harris' attempted jack move left me seeking revenge and I was determined to get it. Two days after the initial discovery of the crack cocaine, the six of us were all taken back to the Federal Courthouse in downtown Atlanta for individual debriefings of the incident conducted by members of the USMS.

It was after being placed back together in a USP ATL holding cell to await the arrival of the transporting Deputy US Marshals that inmate Ziplag chronologically detailed the events leading up to and during the confiscation. During debriefing, they introduced camera recorded surveillance footage revealing that the Ziploc® bag had been purposefully discarded by another detainee taken into custody by the USMS earlier that day, prior to our arrival. So, not to say that it was planted intentionally, but it was clear to me at this point that there was no escaping detection of the act of picking it up and inmate Ziplag stashing it on his person. In his ZIPLAG pick up, he also picked up drug possession charges and an additional introduction of contraband charge for bringing the crack cocaine into the prison.

To my knowledge, the rest of the matter pertaining to the ZIPLAG incident was swept under the rug in an effort to cover up the action and inaction of Deputy "David," the elderly US Marshal, who seemingly had planted the crack in the first place. Oh I'm sorry, did I say that?!

Exhibit B-1

ORIGINAL

IN THE UNITED STATES DISTRICT COURT

FOR THE NORTHERN DISTRICT OF GEORGIA_9JUL-1

ATLANTA DIVISION

(NITED STATES OF AMERICA   :
                                  : CRIMINAL ACTION
                                  :
    NO. 1:90-CR-266 GREGORY   : HARRIS
                                  :

MOTION TO REDUCE SENTENCE

Comes now the United States of America, by Kent B. Alexander, United States Attorney, and John S. Davis, Assistant United States Attorney for the Northern District of Georgia, and moves to reduce the sentence of defendant Gregory Harris, as follows:

The defendant was convicted in this cocaine conspiracy case on February 12, 1992, and was sentenced on May 8, 1992, to 292 months imprisonment. The court of appeals affirmed the conviction. United States v. Harris, 20 F.3d 445 (11th Cir. 1994).

The defendant, who began cooperating with the government beginning in about July 1993, has provided substantial assistance in the investigation and prosecution of other persons. Moreover, at least a portion of the defendant s assistance involved information and evidence not known by the defendant until more than one year after imposition of sentence. See Fed. R. crim. P. 35 (b). Accordingly, the government hereby moves for a 33% reduction (98 months, with a resulting sentence of 194 months) in the defendant s sentence of imprisonment. The defendant's assistance is summarized below.

Beginning in July 1993, working primarily with DEA case agent Ron Geer, the defendant submitted to debriefings involving the instant case, as well as a number of related drug cases. The defendant was interviewed by Al-TSA^ts Buddy Parker, Jim Martin, and Candie Howard, and testified in several grand jury investigations, including those involving Thomas Pressley & Chad Clowers (see below) , Kenny Miles (see below) , Al Brown, and defendants involved in the Fred Tokars investigation .

The defendant made several attempts to work proactively with DEA agents. In one instance, the defendant arranged for two of his associates to come to DEA to be debriefed and to cooperate with agents

42

37

on the defendant's behalf. The two associates soon became unavailable and were later discovered to have turned against the defendant and to have informed other drug dealers that the defendant was cooperating with the government. The defendant s girlfriend also submitted to debriefings in an effort to assist the government. The defendant's girlfriend was contacted by DEA agents on two occasions but was not heard from again. DEA received information that the girlfriend had advised other drug dealers that the defendant was cooperating. These developments prevented the defendant from undertaking proactive cases for a time.

The defendant continued to seek ways to assist the government. The defendant referred Reginald Crawford, Germaine Powell, and Dennis Kens ley to DEA agents, who later debriefed them. The defendant also succeeded in encouraging inmates to contact DEA Agent Geer about cooperating with the government. Agent Geer referred inmates to the offices and agents responsible for their cases.

In June 1995 the defendant contacted Agent Geer about a firearms dealer who was selling illegal weapons. The defendant worked with ATF in an effort to set up a controlled buy of illegal weapons. ATF had previously been aware of the target and expressed an interest in pursuing an active investigation. The defendant spoke to ATF agents and made consensual calls from prison at their direction. Through no fault of the defendant, the case against the gun dealer did not materialize.

In July 1995, Kenneth Miles was arrested on a warrant from the Southern District of Georgia. Miles had been a drug target in this District since 1989. The defendant subsequently provided important grand jury testimony against Miles and was a critical part of the effort to persuade Miles to cooperate with the government, and to enter a guilty plea in the Southern District and thereby avoid additional charges in this District. Miles has since testified in at least two federal cases and has been debriefed several times by agents in Atlanta and Savannah.

In September 1995, the defendant made consensual telephone calls to Tracy Little, a known drug dealer. The defendant made several calls to set up a potential transaction, and also introduced an undercover agent to Little over the telephone. A copy of Agent Geer's DEA—6, prepared on March 11, 1996, and describing telephone calls made by the defendant to the Little organization, is Attachment A to this Motion. A HIDTA task force agent was assigned to follow up on the calls and the investigation, but nothing was done until January 1996. In that month, Little was arrested in a "reverse" operation essentially identical to the one that the defendant had set up in September 1995. AUSA Catherine

43

O 'Neil prosecuted the case. The defendant was considered to be a key witness in the case against Little and his co—defendant, Demetrius Brownlee. The government used the defendant 's debriefing for purposes of establishing drug quantities in the Little conspiracy; because of the defendant ' s statements, which corroborated those of another cooperating witness, the government was able to attribute a significant quantity of cocaine to Little. In addition, the undercover telephone call that the defendant made was part of the discovery in the case and may have had some impact on the two defendants' eventual decisions to plead guilty. Little later cooperated with the government.

In December 1995 the defendant testified in a retrial in the Middle District of Georgia against Fredel Williamson, prosecuted by AUSA Mike Solis. The defendant's testimony against Williamson was accurate and credible; he said that he had obtained between five and eight kilograms of cocaine per week from Williamson, totaling 200 to 300 kilos. Kenny Miles also testified in the Williamson trial, and Williamson was convicted on all three counts.

In United States v. Thomas Pressley, a large cocaine conspiracy prosecuted in this District by AUSA Jim Martin, the defendant twice appeared as a witness. The defendant was debriefed on the Pressley drug ring in October 1993, and, on May 4, 1994, the defendant testified before the grand jury. About a year later, Pressley and four other defendants (including Chad C lowers) were indicted for being part of a continuing criminal enterprise which began in May 1989 and continued through the date of the indictment. The defendant provided information and testimony as to all five named defendants in Pressley.

On October 30, 1996, the defendant testified in Pressley's trial. (The other four defendants had already pleaded guilty.) The defendant and another unindicted coconspirator were the last witnesses called. The defendant again described his drug activity with the Pressley conspiracy from 1988 until January 1992, when he was arrested in the instant case. The defendant established that he had delivered twenty to thirty kilograms of cocaine to Pressley and helped to show that Pressley was a principal organizer and leader in the enterprise. The defendant ᵗ s testimony also furthered the government's theory that two businesses operated by Pressley and a co—defendant, Earnest Hill, were, in fact, fronts for Hill ᵗ s and Pressley ᵗ s drug dealings. Pressley was convicted on all counts and, as of March 1997, was awaiting sentencing; he faced a mandatory life sentence.

Although most of the defendant's assistance to the government involved information already known by the defendant at the time of his 1992 sentencing hearing, the telephone calls made in September 1995 in the Tracy Little investigation yielded evidence and information not known by the defendant until more than one year after imposition of sentence. The defendant therefore is eligible to receive a reduction of his sentence under Rule 35 (b). The government requests that the Court, in considering the instant motion, consider all of the assistance provided by the defendant to the government, and not merely his assistance in the Little case.

Finally, because public knowledge of the defendant s cooperation with the government might pose a risk to the defendant, the United Court requests that this Motion, and any resulting action by the Court, be placed under seal.

WHEREFORE, the United States respectfully requests that this Honorable Court:

     (A)   Schedule a hearing on the instant motion;

     (B)   Upon hearing, order, pursuant to Rule 35 (b) of the Federal Rules of Criminal Procedure, that the defendant ' s sentence be reduced by 98 months, with a resulting final sentence of 194 months;

     (C)   Seal this Motion, and any action thereon by the Court; and

     (D) Grant such further relief as is just.

Respectfully submitted,

KENT B. ALEXANDER
UNITED STATES ATTORNEY

JOHN S. DAVIS
ASSISTANT UNITED STATES ATTORNEY

1800 U.S. Courthouse
75 Spring St., S. W.
Atlanta, GA 30335 404/581-6017
Georgia Bar No. 211060

U.S. Department of Justice
Drug **Enforcement**Administration

REPORT OF INVESTIGATION

Page 1 of 3

1. PROGRAM CODE	2. CROSS RELATED FILES FILE	3. FILE NO. G3-%-0157	4. G-DEP IDENTIFIER HGCID
⁵ BY: S/A Ronald Geer AT: Atlanta, Ga.	G3-89-0035 ☐ ☐	S. FILE TITLE LI'ITLE, Tracy et. al.	
7. Closed Requested Action Completed Action Requested B :		8. DATE PREPARED March 11, 1996	

9. OTHER OFFICERS:
S/A Charles Metzger, TFA Brian Anderson, NS SA Daniel Arrugeta

10.REPORT RE:
Conversations with Tracy LITIIE and acquisition of exhibits N23 and N24

SYNOPSIS:

Attempts were made to contact Tracy LITTLE at his residence via the telephone in order to introduce an undercover agent to him. The undercover agent was to offer cocaine for sale. Several calls were monitored/recorded between Gregory HARRIS and Tracy LITTLE and others.

DETAILS:

1. In September 1995, SA Geer received information from a confidential source (CS) concerning the drug trafficking activities of Tracy LITTLE and others. The CS advised that Greg HARRIS was attempting to contact T. LITTLE in an effort to introduce him to a source for cocaine. In late September, SA Geer began to monitor and record telephone calls between Gregory HARRIS and individuals at telephone number 404/349-7305.

2. Intelligence information revealed that G. HARRIS had supplied T. LITIIE with cocaine during the late 1980's and into the early 1990's. HARRIS was a multi kilogram cocaine trafficker who moved up to 60 kilograms of cocaine a month. HARRIS was convicted under G3-89-0035 on conspiracy to distribute cocaine charges. HARRIS was sentenced to 24 years in federal prison and was designated to the Federal Correctional Facility in Jessup, Ga. The calls from G. HARRIS which were monitored and recorded by SA Geer were made from the FCI in Jessup, Ga.

3. The following is a synopsis of calls made by G. HARRIS to 404/349-7305. The calls were monitored, recorded by SA Geer and subsequently processed as exhibit N-23:

     a)   9-28-95 / 1:10 pm

G. HARRIS called 404/349-7305 and spoke to a subject identified only as "DUKE
. G. HARRIS was told that T. LITTLE had just left. DUKE told HARRIS that LITTLE was out on the street and that he would probably not be in for the rest of the day. HARRIS told DUKE that he would call back later in the day that he was going to have his man 'Carlos' contact T. LITTLE.

(May

41

11. DISTRIBUTION: REGION	12. SIGNATURE (Agent) S A Ronald Geer I	13. DATE 3-14-96
DISTRICT Atlanta-DIG	14. APPROVED (Name and Tide)	15. DATE 3-14-96
OTHER SARI DOE	GIS William D. Hudson III	

DEA Form
1 990)   DEA se.8smvEC)   DRUG ENFORCEMENT ADMINISTRATION
THC   t is the property of the Drug Enforcement Administration.
Is   ontents may be disseminated outside the agency to which loaned.   r•ptt
Noit— it me its 3   Previous edition may be used.

Originatin

Attachment "A"

REPORT OF INVESTIGATION (Continuation	1. FILE NO. G3-96-0157	2. G-DEP IDENTIFIER HGCID
	3. FILE TITLE LITILE, Tracy et. al.	
4. Page 2 of 3		
S. PROGRAM CODE	S. DATE PREPARED March 11, 1996	

b)   9-28-95 / 1:23 pm

G. HARRIS called 404/349-7305 and spoke to DUKE   who advised that T. LITTLE had not returned home. A second subject by the name of 'BRADLEY' spoke to HARRIS briefly. They discussed his living with T. LITILE, DUKE and a subject by the name of Dirk. The phone was returned to DUKE who told G. HARRIS that he spoke to T. LITILE and delivered G. HARRIS's message. DUKE and G. HARRIS discussed the availability of cocaine. DUKE mentioned that business was slow in Herndon Homes. During the conversation, G. HARRIS told DUKE that he wanted to introduce his man Carlos to T. LITTLE, G. HARRIS explained that Carlos was his source of supply. G. HARRIS told DUKE that he would call back tomorrow.

c)   9-29-95 / 2:45 pm

G. HARRIS called 404/349-7305 and spoke to DUKE. G. HARRIS was told that T. IXITLE had left and was at Herndon Homes, in the projects. told G. HARRIS that T. LITILE was expecting his call earlier in the day. DUKE stated that T. LITTLE was out "handling his business' and that he did not how when he was to return. G. HARRIS and DUKE had general conversation. DUKE told HARRIS that he was out trying to make a dollar. call was terminated with HARRIS telling DUKE that he would call T. LITTLE earlier the next day.

d)   9-3W5 / 9:38 am

G. HARRIS   404/349-7305 and poke to Tracy 111TLE. HARRIS told T. ü'1T1.E that he was going to give his source of cocaine (Carlos) LITTLE's pager   HARRIS told LITTLE that he would have Carlos put in his (HARRIS's) code of #99. HARRIS stated that Carlos could beat the price LI'ITLE was currently paying for cocaine. T. LITI'LE and G. HARRIS briefly discussed general topics and T. LITTLE's business in Herndon Homes. T. LI'ITLE stated that he was doing okay   and that he was able to put a dollar in his pocket and pay his bills. HARRIS and LITTLE discussed other subjects who were known to be in the drug business, some of whom were in prison. LITII,E also mentioned the Atlanta Police corruption involving a police offer by the street name of Pac-man. HARRIS asked T. LITTLE to send him money to be put on his telephone account and that he would have Carlos call him on his pager.

4. The following is a synopsis of a conversation between INS SA Daniel Arrugeta and Tracy LITTLE concerning a meeting to discuss. LITTLE purchasing a quantity of cocaine. The tape was processed as exhibit N-24.

a)   10-495 / 10:22 am

(May

42

At approximately 10:20 am, SA D. Arrugeta placed a call to pager number 404/341-0289 with a code of *99. This pager number was obtained from G HARRIS. Approximately 2 minutes later, a return call was placed to the Group 1 undercover telephone. A subject who identified himself as Tracy (LITIIE) was on the telephone. SA Arrugeta told T. LITII.E that was Greg's friend and that he was in town on business. SA Arrugeta stated that he understood tut T LITTLE may be interested in purchasing some "oil" (kilogram of cocaine.) SA Arrugeta asked T. LITTLE how much may be interested in. T. LITTLE stated that he would be interested in one half can of oil.

DEA SENSMVE

3

REPORT OF INVESTIGATION (Continuation)	1. FILE NO. G396-0157	2. G-DEP IDENTIFIER HGCID
	3. FILE TITLE LITTLE, Tracy et. al.	
4. Page 3 of 3		
5. PROGRAM CODE	e. DATE PREPARED March 11,	

When SA Arrugeta told T. LITTLE that thought bethought LITTLE going to obtain more than one half can of oil, T. LITTLE told SA Arrugeta that he would possibly be interested in more but that he would like to meet and talk first. T. LITTLE and SA Arrugeta made arrangements to meet 10-5-95 at 11:00 am on North Avenue in front of The Varsity. T. LITTLE described himself as being 6'4', 200 pounds and stated would be wearing army fatigues.

5.   On 10-5-95 agents responded to the area of The Varsity in preparation for the 11 am meeting between Tracy LITTLE and SA D. Arrugeta. Agents waited until after 12:00 noon with no sign of T. LI'ITLE. An attempt to contact T. LITI'LE vas made via telephone with negative results. The tape recorder malfunctioned during the call thus no recording was made. Information later received from a confidential source indicated that T. LITLE got involved in an unrelated errand and was unable to make the meeting with SA Arrugeta. TFA Brian Anderson was to make additional attempts to coordinate a meeting between SA Arrugeta and T. LI'ITLE.

CUSTODY OF EVIDENCE:

Exhibit N-23 is a cassette tape with telephone conversations recorded on 9-28-95, 9-29-95 and 9-3()-95 between Gregory HARRIS and other individuals at #404/349-7305. N-24 is a cassette tape of a conversation recorded on 104-95 between INS SA D. Arrugeta and Tracy LI'ITLE. N-23 and N-24 were maintained in the custody of SA Geer and subsequently processed as evidence under this file number. exhibits were released to the Atlanta D.O. Non-Drug Evidence Custodian.

NDEXD.IG SECTION:

1. HARRIS, Gregory   NADDIS #2256498
2. 11TILE, Tracy NADDIS #3010437

(May

DEA arm

1990) - 60

DEA SENSMVE

DRUG ENFORCEMENT ADMINISTRATION

This report is the property of the Drug Enforcement Administration.
Neither it nor its contents may be disseminated outside the agency to which loaned.

3

CERTIFICATE OF SERVICE

Previous edition may be used.

(May

Episode VI

Close Call — War of Writs

Months after the conclusion of the ZIPLAG incident (1998) and between the hours 8:00 and 10:00 AM, USP Atlanta prison guards informed me that I needed to go pack up all my personal belongings because I was leaving USP Atlanta that morning to be flown via FBP aircraft back to USP Leavenworth. A little unpublished minor detail, the "writ" that brought me back to Atlanta from Leavenworth had been lifted, requiring the FBP to place me on transit status back to USP Leavenworth. Normally, on FBP inmate shipping days during the transfer process, the use of the inmate telephone system in DCU-2 Housing Unit is prohibited for security reasons surrounding transport details.

However, on the morning that I was to be transported back to USP Leavenworth, I was able to sneak and make a very brief call to a family member, despite the brevity and security risk. On that call, I provided her with the office telephone number of Assistant U.S. Attorney Catherine O'Neal, who, at the time, was assigned to my Fed-case and also responsible for the "writ" that had originally brought me back to Atlanta from Leavenworth. After providing the family member with Catherine O'Neal's office telephone number, I then instructed her to waste no time in calling Catherine O'Neal and inform her that I was currently in the process of preparing to be shipped back to USP Leavenworth, and if I was to return there, my life would be in immediate and grave danger as a result of my involvement in the crack cocaine (ZIPLAG) incident. Even though that family member had carried out my instructions precisely and immediately after ending the brief phone call from me, my cooperation with the government and my becoming a "snitch" remained below the snitching radar, a secret to all save those I interacted with for that sole purpose until the publication of the USA Today Newspaper article in living color photo starring yours truly.

In response to the phone call, Catherine O'Neal issued another "writ" immediately, keeping me in Atlanta (thank God), and she also had the USMS contact USP Atlanta with instructions to bring my shipping process to a screeching halt. Of course there were conditions; pending continued cooperation (snitching) and re-designation, but I was good with that. Given that I snitched concerning inmate Ziplag, who was serving time at USP Leavenworth, as was I, a separation order was issued keeping the two of us apart indefinitely for the remainder of our prison sentences. Luckily for me, by that time, inmate Ziplag had already been returned to USP Leavenworth from the "writ" that had previously brought him back to Atlanta. For the aforementioned reasons, I never returned to Leavenworth.

Episode VII

Stacking the Deck — Snitch my Bitch — Wire Tap

It was now 1998, and I was still being housed in DCU-2 Housing Unit of USP Atlanta, even though my cooperation with the government regarding the PBG, other unrelated individuals, and matters of consideration had already assured me a Rule 35 Sentence Reduction in the near future. As a means of strengthening the Rule 35 Sentence Reduction that I eventually received, I was abundantly forthcoming with relevant information to FLEAs and members of the Atl-USAO as well as a wealth of other forms of cooperation. Remember, I had a prison sentence of over seventeen years that I desperately needed to reduce. If I saw it, heard about it, or knew something beneficial to my mission, I reported it like an ambitious, overzealous journalist without hesitation.

It was also in 1998 that I potentially would get the revenge that I sought against inmate Gregory Harris for his previous actions, or at least I thought I would get the sought-after revenge. During the span of my continued cooperation, the "writ" that brought Gregory Harris back to Atlanta from a Federal Prison located in Estill, South Carolina was lifted, returning him back to that Federal prison to continue serving out his Federal Prison Sentence.

While in each other's presence as DCU-2 dorm orderlies, "ViralInmateInfo.com" alerted me that inmate Harris was selling information pertaining to a Fed-case on its way to trial to inmates who were either already cooperating with or needing and wanting to cooperate with the government. The price tag? Five-thousand dollars a pop! Yes, selling government information is profitable beyond your imagination, because almost every federal detainee is seeking help to receive a sentencing reduction. The Federal case in question was United States v. Terrence Franklin (Case No, 1:97-CR-179-ODE-GGB), in which Atlanta based attorney, Donald F. Samuel, was the Defense Attorney representing Defendant Terrence Franklin during one of the 1998 debriefings. I reported Gregory Harris' actions to the FLEAs and members of the Atl-USAO conducting the debriefing.

So what was it that made me bring that matter to the attention of the federal agents and representatives from the Atl-USAO? My desire for revenge was first and foremost on the agenda, but, also, it was the fact that the inmates purchasing the information were being prepared by Harris himself to testify as government witnesses in the US v. Franklin Federal case. Little did I know at the time, his actions were sanctioned by FLEAs and members of the Atl-USAO involved in the case and that Gregory Harris was an active member of their inner circle. When I was later accepted to the inner circle, I was clued in that the practice he was using to assemble government witnesses is technically known as "**Stacking the Deck**" and is a very common practice used by local FLEAs and Atl-USAO to secure (fraudulent) indictments and convictions.

Weeks after informing the two agencies of Harris' actions, I was brought over for another debriefing and asked to wear a wire at USP Atlanta for the sole purpose of recording a conversation between myself and one of the inmates buying the government shared information Harris was selling and debriefing the inmates on. I agreed to wear the wire without thought. Like I shared previously, I was ready to serve however it benefited my mission. By the time of that particular debriefing, I had become mentally and sexually bored of Mrs. Grayer. It was just a dull routine repeating itself bla..bla..bla..bla..bla so, I decided to sacrifice her at that debriefing as well, reporting our romantic sexual relationship to both agencies in attendance.

The environment in which I grew up taught me at an early age that females were no different than the food items that you purchase at a grocery store. They are both consumable commodities with a limited shelf life; females have an expiration date. Yes, this may offend some readers, but we all are groomed differently in our upbringing, this is how I was taught, although not by my grandparents. In my defense, it was more of what I witnessed about relationships in the streets than word of mouth. My grandfather respected, honored and treated my grandmother like an irreplaceable Queen, which I will always love and appreciate him for. Not only did my grandmother have 13 kids, who never went a day hungry, never were forced to wear too little or old clothes due to a lack of money, but on account of my grandfather's ability to provide as a man (a black man at that during challenging times) my grandmother never worked a day in her life and owned her house. I miss the both of them so much.

So back to the story, the inmate in question, the target of me wearing the wire, went by the name, Randy Lee Baynes, aka "Rock." A black male over six feet tall and outweighing me by over a hundred pounds, Rock had a full gold grill. I on the other hand was only 5'5" and weighed no more than 175 pounds then. When trying to visualize inmate Baynes, just picture a black version of "Jaws" with the full silver grill in the old James Bond movies, "The Spy Who Loved Me" and "Moonraker" — yeah, that guy.

In less than a week after agreeing to wear the wire, it was show time for me again, and on that day, I was escorted to an administration office within the prison's walls where the two federal agents from the previous debriefing awaited my arrival. It wasn't unusual activity for me to be seen wandering around outside of the DCU-2 Housing Unit with Mrs. Grayer, but she was about to become a ghost, getting greyer and greyer, so it may as well had been on this occasion. Nonetheless, it was my fading glory, my expiring consumable, Mrs. Grayer, who escorted me to the awaiting federal agents.

After arriving at the office where the two federal agents awaited, which just so happened to be the office that Mrs. Grayer and I had sex in on numerous occasions, the two federal agents informed Mrs. Grayer that her assistance was needed, and that wasn't out of the ordinary either. So she agreed, anticipating that I was "coming home" to her and aware of the fact that these actions would expedite my return home to her. Such a drab (gray) way of envisaging "HOME or A TRUE LOVE AFFAIR", don't you think? But then again, we're talking about Mrs. Grayer — pun definitely intended. In light of this (oxymoron), she was a willing participant during the entire process.

Unbeknownst to Mrs. Grayer, these same two federal agents were investigating her and would be confronting her with their findings in the weeks to come. Having secured Mrs. Grayer's assistance, the two federal agents went to work placing the wire and recorder on my body and training me on the use of the equipment. I had 90 minutes of tape and a toggle switch for on/off control by the host, me. Mrs. Grayer then escorted me to the housing unit accommodating inmate Randy Baynes. Mrs. Grayer went about business as usual, and I went in search of my victim. Sorry Charlie! When I found inmate Baynes, I informed him that I needed to speak to him in private, to which he quickly agreed. He and I had already engaged in several one-on-one conversations pertaining to snitching and being granted sentence reductions, so I knew he wouldn't have a problem agreeing to speak to me in the privacy of his cell.

Once alone with him, I smoothly turned on the recorder and went straight to work, memorializing the requisite information and unrelated but insightful information as a bonus. He not only talked about Gregory Harris' selling of information and of his own purchases of detailed information key to the United States v. Terrence Franklin court case, but he disclosed so much non-solicited criminal and incriminating activity that I had to turn the recorder off. That whole encounter was very sneaky, enlightening and entertaining, but now, time to find the 'Grayer' side of life: time to go.

After recording Randy Baynes' sought-after knowledge and spill-over, I linked up with Mrs. Grayer, and we headed back to the administration office where the two federal agents were awaiting my return. Once back in the privacy of the administration office, the two federal agents asked me if I was successful in my quest to extract the requisite information, to which I quickly affirmed. Undercover prisoner and successful! They then proceeded to remove the wire device and instructed the uber-clueless Mrs. Grayer to return me to my assigned housing unit while they departed USP Atlanta. With her expectation of me coming home to her soon, my sleeper play on the snitching field would lay her up for a 'nude' awakening, just not the type of homecoming nudity she expected. How rude, right? Like they say, "Don't hate the playa, hate the game."

Weeks after I wore the wire baiting Randy Baynes, I was brought back over to the Atl-USAO for a debriefing pertaining to the wire escapade and the taboo of realizing a sexual fantasy gone gray with Mrs. Grayer. The debriefing was conducted by the same two federal agents and representatives from Atl-USAO. Regarding my wire gig, everyone in attendance, including me, listened to my recorded conversation with inmate Randy Baynes via headphones for the purpose of me interpreting the slang words used.

Wintry months after that 1998 debriefing, inmate Harris was brought back to Atlanta on another "writ" which ultimately resulted in federal obstruction of justice charges being filed against him and Randy Baynes, case number 1:99-CR-684-GET-ECS. (See following Exhibit B-2) Another mission achieved and payback for trying to play me.

Also, during that same period of time, Mrs. Grayer experienced her nude awakening as she was stripped of her job, fired as a result of me exposing our sexual frolicking. To avoid prosecution, Mrs. Grayer admitted to being sexually involved with me when confronted with the evidence against her. I know. What an asshole, right? As I told you before, I wasn't just a male inmate voluntarily exposing his sexual tango with a woman on the payroll. At this point, I was a dedicated servant for our U.S government: A snitch seeking all aspects of personal gain. Look, I realize that no matter the case, it is somewhat shocking and maybe incredible, as in not credible, but I take your thoughts back to "Ripley's Believe or Not!®." Stranger things have happened, believe me. Just add it to the episodes of "Stranger Things X". You see it clearly from my point of view with my next utterance.

Once I crossed over and broke the code of silence, relishing my integrity, and willing to bury anyone who tried to rob me of such honor associated with being a "snitch," I did so with a 'by any means necessary,' cut throat mentality. Furthermore, fuckin' wit Mrs. Grayer and all the shit we was doin' was fuckin' up my damn rehabilitation efforts. Bitch had to go (lol)! Bon voyage to my Ex-sex. Next! Yeah, that homie. The next day, I was transferred out of USP Atlanta for safety reasons draped in the robe of my latest snitch-work, "staff shaft," and wiretap.

Just as Mrs. Grayer was presented with the evidence against her, the same occurred with inmates Gregory Harris and Randy Baynes. One more round of separation orders pleeeeaaaase! Step right up, get your separation order here and now! I'm thinking I might need it issued pronto to keep me separated from inmates Gregory Harris and Randy Baynes... indefinitely, and you know the rest. All at once!...for the remainder of my incarceration.

Exhibit B-2

CLOSED

U.S. District Court
Northern District of Georgia (Atlanta)
CRIMINAL DOCKET FOR CASE #: 1:99-cr-00684-GET-ECS All Defendants

Case title: USA v. Baynes, et al

Date Filed: 12/08/1999
Date Terminated: 07/13/2000

Assigned to: Judge G. Ernest Tidwell
Referred to: Magistrate Judge E.
Clayton Scofield, III

Defendant (1)

Randy Lee Baynes
TERMINATED: 07/13/2000

represented by **Joseph M. Winter**
Alembik Fine & Callner
245 Peachtree Center Avenue, N.E.
Marquis One Tower, Fourth Floor
Atlanta, GA 30303
404-688-8800
TERMINATED: 07/13/2000
LEAD ATTORNEY
ATTORNEY TO BE NOTICED
Designation: CJA Appointment

Pending Counts

18:371.F CONSPIRACY TO
DEFRAUD THE UNITED STATES
(1)

Disposition

CNT 1: CBOP 15 mos to be served consecutive
to sentence dft now serving – 3 yrs supv'd
release – $100 special assessment. *4/19/01:
Sentence reduced to 10 months per order*

Highest Offense Level (Opening)

Felony

Terminated Counts

18:1503.F INFLUENCE/INJURING
OFFICER/JUROR/WITNESS
(2)

18:1001.F STATEMENTS OR
ENTRIES GENERALLY
(3-4)

Disposition

Dismissed counts on govt motion.

Dismissed counts on govt motion.

Highest Offense Level (Terminated)

Felony

Complaints

None

Disposition

Assigned to: Judge G. Ernest Tidwell
Referred to: Magistrate Judge E.
Clayton Scofield, III

Defendant (2)

Gregory Vernon Harris
TERMINATED: 07/12/2000

represented by **Steven Paul Berne**
Law Offices of Steven Berne

		mag/judge) (bh) (Entered: 01/04/2000)
12/23/1999	5	ORDER by Mag Judge John E. Dougherty as to defendant Gregory Vernon Harris, Appointing Steven Paul Berne as Counsel (cc/served by mag/judge) (bh) (Entered: 01/04/2000)
12/23/1999	6	ARRAIGNMENT HELD before Mag Judge John E. Dougherty . Case assigned to Judge G. E. Tidwell . Pretrial referral to Mag Judge E. C. Scofield III as to Gregory Vernon Harris PLEA OF NOT GUILTY. (bh) (Entered: 01/04/2000)
12/28/1999	7	Pretrial order setting pretrial conference for 1/12/00 10:00 by Mag Judge E. C. Scofield III as to defendant Gregory Vernon Harris, c/served by mag/judge (bh) (Entered: 01/04/2000)
01/06/2000	8	MOTION by defendant Gregory Vernon Harris for continuance of pretrial conference (bh) (Entered: 01/10/2000)
01/07/2000	9	MOTION by defendant Gregory Vernon Harris to extend time to file pretrial motions and [8-1] motion for continuance of pretrial conference , to continue pretrial conference (bh) (Entered: 01/10/2000)
01/19/2000	10	ORDER by Mag Judge E. C. Scofield III as to defendant Gregory Vernon Harris GRANTING [9-1] motion to extend time to file pretrial motions to 2/18/00 and [8-1] motion for continuance of pretrial conference to 2/2/00 at 10:00, GRANTING [9-2] motion to continue pretrial conference, GRANTING [8-1] motion for continuance of pretrial conference, and to exclude pursuant to 18:3161(h)(8)(A)(B) beginning 12/23/99 and ending 2/2/00 (cc:served by mag/judge) (bh) (Entered: 01/25/2000)
01/19/2000	11	MOTION by defendant Gregory Vernon Harris for preservation of agents' notes (bh) (Entered: 01/25/2000)
01/19/2000	12	MOTION by defendant Gregory Vernon Harris for government notice of intent to use evidence arguably subject to suppression with brief in support. (bh) (Entered: 01/25/2000)
01/19/2000	13	MOTION by defendant Gregory Vernon Harris for disclosure of impeachment information with brief in support. (bh) (Entered: 01/25/2000)
01/19/2000	14	MOTION by defendant Gregory Vernon Harris for access to prospective government witnesses with brief in support. (bh) (Entered: 01/25/2000)
01/19/2000	15	PRELIMINARY MOTION by defendant Gregory Vernon Harris to suppress (bh) (Entered: 01/25/2000)
01/19/2000	16	MOTION by defendant Gregory Vernon Harris for severance with brief in support. (bh) (Entered: 01/25/2000)
01/19/2000	17	MOTION by defendant Gregory Vernon Harris for an order requiring the prosecution to give notice of its intention to rely upon other crimes evidence (bh) (Entered: 01/25/2000)
01/19/2000	18	MOTION by defendant Gregory Vernon Harris to file additional motions and to supplement motions (bh) (Entered: 01/25/2000)
01/19/2000	19	MOTION by defendant Gregory Vernon Harris for discovery and inspection (bh) (Entered: 01/25/2000)
01/19/2000	21	INITIAL APPEARANCE HEARING held for Randy Lee Baynes before Mag Judge E. C. Scofield III . (pt) (Entered: 02/04/2000)
01/19/2000	22	ARRAIGNMENT HELD before Mag Judge E. C. Scofield III . Case assigned to Judge G. E. Tidwell . Pretrial referral to Mag Judge E. C. Scofield III as to Randy Lee Baynes PLEA OF NOT GUILTY. (pt) (Entered: 02/04/2000)
01/19/2000	23	ORDER by Mag Judge E. C. Scofield III as to defendant Randy Lee Baynes, Appointing Brian Mendelsohn (for IA only) Public Defender as Counsel (cc) (pt) (Entered: 02/04/2000)
01/27/2000	20	Motion by USA as to Randy Lee Baynes, Gregory Vernon Harris for continuance of pretrial conference (pt) (Entered: 01/31/2000)

		custody of USM. Signed by Judge G. E. Tidwell (cc:USA,USM,USPO,PSA,DFT,CNSL,FIN) (pt) (Entered: 07/14/2000)
07/13/2000		Case terminated. (pt) (Entered: 07/14/2000)
07/13/2000	38	GOVERNMENT MOTION TO DISMISS COUNTS and ORDER GRANTING same by Judge G. E. Tidwell as to Randy Lee Baynes (1) count(s) 2, 3 –4 . (cc: USA, USM, USPO, CNSL, DFT) (pt) (Entered: 07/14/2000)
07/14/2000	39	MOTION by USA as to Gregory Vernon Harris and ORDER GRANTING substitution of custody by Mag Judge E. C. Scofield III (bsm) (Entered: 07/20/2000)
07/27/2000		Return of service executed 7/26/00 as to Gregory Vernon Harris. Cert cys of this docment mailed to FCI, Estill, SC. (pt) (Entered: 07/28/2000)
08/01/2000		Steno notes of proceedings held as to defendant Randy Lee Baynes 7/13/00 before Judge G. E. Tidwell , by Court Reporter Pat M. Tanner. (mrb) (Entered: 08/04/2000)
08/01/2000		Steno notes of proceedings held as to defendant Gregory Vernon Harris 7/12/00 before Judge G. E. Tidwell , by Court Reporter Pat M. Tanner. (mrb) (Entered: 08/04/2000)
08/08/2000		Return of service executed 8/2/00 as to Gregory Vernon Harris. Dft delivered to FCI, Estill, SC (pt) (Entered: 08/09/2000)
08/11/2000		Return of service executed 8/11/00 as to Randy Lee Baynes. Dft delivered to FCI, Yazoo City, MS. (pt) (Entered: 08/15/2000)
02/07/2001	40	PETITION by USA as to Gregory Vernon Harris and ORDER by Mag Judge Linda T. Walker substituting custody (bsm) (Entered: 02/08/2001)
03/27/2001	41	Motion by USA as to Randy Lee Baynes for reduction of sentence pursuant to Rule 35 (bsm) (Entered: 03/27/2001)
03/27/2001	42	Motion by USA as to Gregory Vernon Harris for reduction of sentence pursuant to Rule 35 (bsm) (Entered: 03/27/2001)
03/27/2001		SUBMITTED to Judge G. E. Tidwell as to defendant Randy Lee Baynes on [41–1] motion for reduction of sentence pursuant to Rule 35 (bsm) (Entered: 03/27/2001)
03/27/2001		SUBMITTED to Judge G. E. Tidwell as to defendant Gregory Vernon Harris on [42–1] motion for reduction of sentence pursuant to Rule 35 (bsm) (Entered: 03/27/2001)
04/19/2001	43	ORDER by Judge G. Ernest Tidwell as to defendant Randy Lee Baynes GRANTING USA's [41–1] motion for reduction of sentence pursuant to Rule 35. Defendant's sentence is reduced by five (5) months, from fifteen (15) to ten (10) months to serve. (cc: USM, USPO, USPS, USA, CNSL, DFT, FIN) (dfb) (Entered: 04/23/2001)
04/19/2001	43	Sentence reduced to 10 months per [43–1] order filed 4/19/01. (dfb) (Entered: 04/23/2001)
04/25/2001		Notice from USM that 2 certified copies of [43–1] order were mailed, cert mail, rrr on 4/24/01 to FCI, Yazoo City, MS. (dfb) (Entered: 04/26/2001)
05/07/2001	44	Response (traverse) by Randy Lee Baynes to [42–1] motion for reduction of sentence pursuant to Rule 35 (bsm) (Entered: 05/08/2001)
05/07/2001	44	MOTION by defendant Randy Lee Baynes to produce evidence in person at Rule 35 hearing with brief in support. (bsm) (Entered: 10/10/2001)
06/06/2001	45	IN–CHAMBERS CONFERENCE HELD before Judge G. E. Tidwell as to defendant Gregory Vernon Harris, govt to withdraw motion for reduction of sentence in this case, and Judge J. Owen Forrester to handle in case pending before him (bsm) (Entered: 06/11/2001)
06/11/2001		Terminated submissions. (bsm) (Entered: 06/11/2001)
10/09/2001	45	Response by USA to [44–1] motion to produce evidence in person at Rule 35 hearing by Randy Lee Baynes (bsm) (Entered: 10/10/2001)

Episode VIII

The Hoax of all Hoaxes — Induction into the World Hall of Shame

After being transferred out of USP Atlanta towards the end of 1998, I was transported via USMS to the Bartow County Jail in Cartersville, Georgia where I spent the next eight to ten months awaiting re-designation. During that time, the Feds had and may still have a contract with the Bartow County Sheriff's Department for the housing of federal inmates at Bartow County Jail. Upon the completion of the re-designation process (summer months of 1999), I was re-designated to USP-Terre Haute, located in Terre Haute, Indiana.

Whereas, I had recently worn a wire on another inmate inside of a high security USP, one would assume that I would have been re-designated to a much safer environment such as a medium security Federal Correctional Institution (FCI) where snitching is acceptable and therefore snitches are welcomed. It was at that time that I started to realize that I had become nothing more than a government pawn, instead of a knight. And even though I had come to that realization, I was in too deep to undo the aftermath of my selfish actions.

Days after being re-designated, I was flown from Atlanta via FBP aircraft to USP Terre Haute. I once again had to endure the dehumanizing intake procedure of being strip-searched, fingerprinted, mug shot. I was then issued linen and clothing before being escorted to my assigned housing unit, "F." Shortly after settling into my new living quarters, I was approached by several of the inmates from my hometown who had actually been awaiting my arrival. But how would they even know that I was en route? Daily, there was a list of names and US Marshal ID numbers of the new arrivals posted within the housing unit. The last three digits of my ID is 019, so they knew that I was either from the city of Atlanta or had caught my Federal Case in Atlanta.

Minutes after the introductions were out of the way, I was informed by these inmates that I would be required to present my pre-sentence investigation report for review by the entire Atlanta "car" (inmates from Atlanta) so that they could confirm whether or not I had received a 5k1.1 Sentence Reduction for snitching on anyone. Even though this didn't occur during my short stay at USP Leavenworth when it still was a high security prison, it is an accepted and commonly required practice for all new arrivals at high security USP's throughout the United States. And when the word "car" is used in such a way within any federal prison of the United States, it simply indicates the city and/or state, or the gang that you and other inmates in that "car" are affiliated with. I had already anticipated that requirement, and given that I had a bench trial and didn't start cooperating with the government until after I was sentenced, I knew my pre-sentence investigation report would be null, nada, nothing, zero. Therefore, it wouldn't state that I received a 5k1.1 Sentence Reduction.

This was crucial, because there have been many violent inmate assaults, some resulting in murders throughout the federal prison system, committed by other inmates after the review of another's pre-sentence investigation report. Naturally, I received approval by the Atlanta car and a welcoming with open arms.

With the knowledge that I would be going back to Atlanta for the purpose of providing more cooperation and eventually receiving my Rule 35 Sentence Reduction, my attorney and I had already agreed upon precautionary measures. In December of 1999 while in the presence of other inmates in the Atlanta car, I received legal mail from my attorney stating that my appeal had been granted, and, therefore, I would be returning to Atlanta within a matter of days. Recalling that I had waived my appeal years ago, the letter that I received was a ruse, a decoy for my protection. This was the precautionary tactic decided and deployed by my attorney. Smart! Two days after I received that fake letter, I was flown back to Atlanta via FBP's aircraft to tend to matters undisclosed.

Having returned to Atlanta from Terre Haute, USMS transported me back to the old APDC in downtown Atlanta, where I had previously been housed under federal custody. Now, at the old APDC, I know you're sick of hearing me say it, but once again dehumanized by the required intake process, I was placed into a housing unit consisting of new federal defendants that were as lame to the ways of the Federal Court System as I was back when I was referred to as a federal defendant instead of federal inmate having been sentenced for the previous four and a half years. Under the circumstances, this was a good look, being housed with new federal defendants that were fresh off the streets with serious bankroll to spend towards their freedom, no matter the cost or route. In the following weeks and months to come, my new Diggs would accommodate a very lucrative and otherwise beneficial future.

Several days after my return, I attended my first debriefing alone, unrepresented and outside of Atl-USAO. By that time I had participated in so many debriefings "dishonorably" that I had established a trustworthy working relationship with not only the HIDTA TF Agents whom were the lead federal agents overseeing all of my cooperation, but the federal agents and members of the Atl-USAO as well. Because of that established honor, my attorney didn't feel the need to be present at every subsequent debriefing. This one was conducted in one of the attorney/client rooms located on the first floor of the old APDC.

I attended numerous debriefings in the attorney/client room, but as an extra incentive for continued outstanding cooperation, federal agents arranged a sexual encounter for me in that same room with a female federal defendant also at that facility. Snitch for a bitch! Nookie for a cookie! Whoomp, there it is! I met her during transport and remained in contact through jailhouse correspondence. It was quite common, actually, during that time to have "staged" conjugal visits, though. FLEAs commonly arranged for the big-time Atlanta drug dealers to have sexual intercourse with their wives, girlfriends, and/or city strippers prior to debriefings. Well, I didn't have a wife, girlfriend, or preferred Cheetah, Onyx, or Magic City stripper to sex up, so I had to settle for sexing some locked up pussy I had met on the wagon. It was my very first time — no, not that first time! I'm referring to the virgin encounter with these particular debriefs composed of agents from the Atl-USAO, HIDTA and FLEA. They immediately disclosed that the federal agent was coincidentally assigned the lead role managing Gregory Harris' cooperation, after which, we got down to business.

It was then and there during that debriefing that I was made a member of the inner circle in the company of inmate Harris, federal agents and members of the Atl-USAO. I'm in, finally. But here's the kicker — pause — Ready? Wait for it! Would you believe me if I told you that them niggas dropped a bomb on me?! Well these niggas dropped a fuckin' bomb on me! I don't know what kind of game these people were playin', but they just hit me wit some real fake ass shit. The entire ordeal of me wearing a wire at USP Atlanta was nothing but a SCAM to cover up and conceal federal agents and members of the Atl-USAO's involvement in the tactics that was being used, i.e. Stacking the Deck. My head is spinning right now, and quite frankly, yours should be too! I'm in a state of shock! Imagine the thoughts running through my veins! I could give a fuck about my head. My whole body was a radiator overheating. What the fuuuck?! So, this 'Stacking the Deck' by inmate Gregory Harris to assemble government witnesses in the US v. Franklin Federal case (Case No, 1:97-CR-179-ODE-GGB) was all a hoax?!!! Maaan, get the fuck outta heeere! I felt stupid!

> *"My radiator can't take it! Frustrated, temper's road ragin'. So many thoughts in my wherever—think it's in my mind, but I'm suspicious. I can't believe what they say to me, 'cause all they ever do is tell lies to me. Everything they taught me in school is sketchy, even the law ain't in my best interest. The jail and the prison system's big business, 11 Wall Street is my witness, I just need a five-minute rain shower, I just needa cool down, man, I just needa cool down!" (Rainshower, Victor Trionfo, 2018)*

I don't know about you, but right now, I need to breathe. I mean, I need some air... My throat is dry and my skin is clammy with it — seems like a rogue shot of heroin racing through my veins right alongside the questionable thoughts. You got me fucked up! Like COVID-19 fucked up!

Pardon me. To the fallen across the globe, victim to COVID-19, the Coronavirus—Rest in Peace, and may God reclaim your soul and heal your loved ones. To those released from federal prisons, state prisons and private facilities all over America due to Coronavirus, kudos. Stay safe—live your life. Show your gratitude in all that you say and do—be thankful for a second chance at life.

Although the federal agents and members of the Atl-USAO involved could not determine if inmates other than myself had also by chance figured out Gregory Harris' actions, my wearing of the wire and the charges filed against Gregory Harris were simply staged as a cover up to conceal all government involvement tangential to the inmate's.

As a result of my interference in "Stacking the Deck" in US v. Franklin, inmate Randy Baynes and several other inmates who had also purchased information from inmate Harris could not be used as government witnesses. Very strange, hard to assimilate amid the hoax ridden episode, Terrence Franklin was acquitted at that trial because of my interference. Huh? What? How is it that my FAKE intervention upset the apple-cart in the actual case. Somebody, some agent, some judge, some official is smoking that Ziplag crack cocaine! Soooo, even though members of Atl-USAO went so far as to actually charge, prosecute, and convict inmate Gregory Harris in regards to the selling of the information, once the dust settled and the smoke cleared, the Atl-USAO did in fact honor their original plea agreement with inmate Gregory Harris by cutting years off his federal prison sentence, and Terrence Franklin walked. Let me get this right. Am I led to believe in all the hype that if I had not interfered, the witnesses would have been admissible in court and the outcome would then have been different? Hmm...

It was at that debriefing that I was given the green light to make the same types of moves that Gregory Harris was allowed to make, and I was instructed on how to best utilize the information that I was receiving from federal agents and that of my external sources for the purpose of financial and other forms of personal gain. To further my worth, I was also taught the methodology of recruiting others into the World Hall of Shame, The Snitching Game....fuck 'cooperation.' Let's call a dragon a dragon. OK, a spade a spade, whatever.

At the conclusion of that debriefing. I felt as though I had become untouchable. I'm the king of the worrrrld! — in federal prison terms, of course. But the future has my name written in the history books of snitching for true personal gain, forever.

Episode IX

Ten Stacks — Criminal Information Sold for Personal Gain

Two weeks after the beginning of the new century, I made my first sale of information actually furnished by HIDTA which I had been cooperating with over the course of four and a half years for the specific purpose of selling. The buyer of the information was a federal defendant fresh off the street who was charged with federal white-collar fraud. I knew that the buyer wouldn't have a problem paying the asking fee of $10,000. Furthermore, being that the source of the information was HIDTA TF Agents, I was confident that the use of the information would instantly breathe success upon the buyer. Just as Gregory Harris had been instructed, I too referred the buyer to the federal agents who had furnished me with information. Assistant U.S. Attorney Catherine O'Neal later made reference to that referral.

Moreover, the timing of the first sale couldn't have been more perfect. When negotiating the sale, the buyer was instructed to have the $10,000 delivered to my daughter's mother at her address. My daughter's mother in turn used $9,000 to purchase new transportation for her and my daughter and use the rest to put money on my books at old ADCP.

Shortly after my first sale of information, I sold the second using information acquired from external sources using the buyer from the first sale as a reference. The second buyer was a well-established drug dealer out of Decatur, Georgia that didn't want to "snitch" on individuals that he knew personally but had no problem snitching on individuals that he had no personal relationship with. He agreed to purchase the needed information pertaining to the latter. I referred the second buyer to the HIDTA TF Agents after making the purchase.

In regards to the use of the information from my first sale, that information was used by the same HIDTA TF Agents that had previously furnished the information to me in an affidavit submitted to a federal judge in Atlanta seeking approval from the judge for a wiretap, which, by the way, was granted based on information that the buyer provided back to those same agents. Do you see the web of entanglement, the vicious, malicious, tainted circle, cycling and recycling of justice, truth, integrity or whatever the hell their motto is? Oh wait, that's like the motto of the crooked USMS...but HIDTA should add to their mission statement..." by any corrupt means possible and necessary." I charged the second buyer of information $10,000 as well. The proceeds from that sale was split equally between my external sources and me, with my half of the money going to my daughter and her mother. I used my third sale, information also furnished to me by HIDTA, that I successfully sold for the same amount, $10,000, which was delivered to free world sources per my instructions. Being that my customers were all in the same housing unit, I didn't think that it would be a smart business decision to charge some less or more than the others. Furthermore, most of my customers during that time were white collar criminals who had stolen large amounts of cash from others. So, a mere $10,000 was pittance.

When I met with the agents to accept the third matter of information, they asked me to contact my external sources to locate a fugitive. Like drones with facial recognition software, I instantly accessed my mind's database with a query that returned the pertinent data and dispensed quickly to them that I would make contact by phone within an hour dictating the coordinates and address of the wanted fugitive. One hour later, I did just that. Amazing is all they could think or say. Assistant U.S. Attorney Catherine O'Neal makes reference of my locating a wanted fugitive to Judge Willis B. Hunt, Jr. during my June 14, 2000 Rule 35 Sentence Reduction Hearing: (See the following Exhibit C-1, page 8 line 21-23 and page 9, line 5-6 of the transcript from the Rule 35 Sentence Reduction Hearing will substantiate Catherine O'Neal's reference).

In regards to the use of the information in my third sale, federal agents had made a huge warrantless, non-probable cause drug bust on some Mexicans, using a technique that I would come to know years later as the "Knock-n-Talk" technique. Therefore, I needed a name other than my own to be used as the confidential source for the information that led up to their use of the "Knock-n-Talk" technique. My job was to find a reliable buyer and provide the buyer with all the furnished information in the event that the buyer had to testify regarding the furnished information during any associated court proceeding.

After successfully negotiating the purchase of information, I referred the buyer to the same agents who then passed the buyer off to the federal agents that had not only actually made the drug bust, but who were members of the agents' inner circle. With three successful sales under my belt, I started educating the buyers of the information and federal snitching defendants within my housing unit. After realizing the significance between the 5k1.1 sentence reduction and the Rule 35 Sentence Reduction, I instructed my students not to provide all of their information pertaining to different individuals and topics of consideration during the 5k1.1 phase. Rather, strategically wait until after sentencing within the required one-year restriction period after sentencing before providing the government with additional information of pertinence. This modus operandi would assure the individual cooperating with the government of the greatest sentence reduction.

At the point of taking necessary actions to secure a 5k1.1 sentence reduction, the defendant faces a degree of uncertainty in regard to the sentencing time adjudicated. However, during the Rule 35 Sentence Reduction process, a defendant has already been sentenced and the point of this follow-up process is to knock more time off the sentence. So, you basically know what level and type of cooperation will be needed to reduce the sentence. Then, what was my angle in educating? I taught defendants on how to outsmart, and how to beat the Federal Court System which in and of itself is corrupt anyway.

Several weeks after I started the sessions, I awoke to eat breakfast one morning with others in my housing unit, surprisingly to find my uncle, "Tall-Face", and his son, "Lil-T", there in the same unit as myself! Unbeknownst to HIDTA, they had staged a bust and pulled up in the Pitt-community the night before and arrested two of my family members using the same corrupt tactics that I fed with the meat and potatoes of stellar support (case no: 1:00-CR-653). But who gave them the drop, because I didn't participate in any way to sell the information used in their arrest. The arrest of my uncle and his son left a bitter taste in my mouth. Again, in full circle, I relapsed with a desire and need for revenge.

A few days after the arrest, during my debriefing with the HIDTA TF Agents, they bragged, laughed, and boasted about the corrupt and illegal tactics that they deployed to arrest and build the case against my uncle and his son. And stated to me that if my uncle's son, "Lil-T", had not snitched on his father, "Tall-Face", then they, HIDTA Agents and the Atl-USAO, would not have had a case against my uncle. Now that's foul! There's no way I could ever snitch on a family member, especially one who had supported and provided for me as Lil-T's father did for him. My father has been absent my entire life and I'd still spare him.

Unbeknownst to me, my cousin "Lil-T" had accepted a cooperation deal with those HIDTA TF Agents and the Atl-USAO and had given incriminating statements against his father, "Tall-Face" in a successful effort to receive his own sentence reduction. I never told the HIDTA TF Agents of my relation to the two individuals that they had arrested that night. As a result of that arrest in 2000, my uncle's federal prison sentence exceeded 20 years, which at the publication of this book was fully served.

His son received a federal prison sentence of 7 years, already served.

Exhibit C-1

Case 1:06-cr-00442-TCB-AJB   Document 209-3   Filed 03/07/16   Page 2 of 4

```
1                    IN THE UNITED STATES DISTRICT COURT

2                   FOR THE NORTHERN DISTRICT OF GEORGIA

3                            ATLANTA DIVISION

4    UNITED STATES OF AMERICA,            )

5                    Plaintiff,           )      Docket No.

6             V.                          )      1:06-CR-442-JEC-LTW

7                                         )      Atlanta, Georgia

8    MARCUS WATKINS,                      )      JANUARY 14, 2000

9                    Defendant,           )

10   _____ )

11                       TRANSCRIPT OF SENTENCING

12            BEFORE THE HONORABLE WILLIS B. HUNT, JR.,

13                   UNITED STATES DISTRICT JUDGE

14

15   APPEARANCES:

16   For the Plaintiff:       CATHERINE O'NEAL, Asst. U. S. Attorney Los Angeles, CA

17

18   For the Defendant:       PAUL KISH, Asst. Federal Defender

19

20   Court Reporter:          Nancy Smith-Wells

21                            United States Courthouse, 312 N. Spring Street, Room 402

22                            Los Angeles, CA 90012   (213) 621-2148

23

24   Proceedings recorded by mechanical stenography, transcript

25   produced by computer.
```

1   Brown of the HIDTA Task Force and with other individuals. He

2   calls me; he calls Assistant United States Attorney Janice

3   Gordon and he calls others to let us know of information that

4   he has learned or that he has found something that he

5   believes would be significant. And I understand, Your Honor,

6   that a lot of defendants do those sort of things because

7   they think that they can just continue to do it to help

8   themselves and obviously Mr. Watkins knows that whatever he

9   does is going to benefit him, but the consistency of his

10 cooperation and the attitude with which he approaches it,

11 Your Honor, in our view exemplifies someone who is also doing

12 it because he truly believes at this point that it is the

13 right thing to do.

14   That information has been significant, intelligence

15 information and other ongoing investigations.

16   Mr. Watkins has also indicated that he wishes to

17 continue to cooperate, even after he is out of custody.

18 Agent Brown is very interested in doing that and pursuing

19 that with him because Mr. Watkins does have an ability to

20 walk the walk and talk the talk and to get in with these

21 individuals and would be a significant source of information.

22   One of the other important things that he has done

23 in these casual conversations, Agent Brown did go over to

24 speak with him at some point in the earlier this year and

25 late last year about some other information and it came to

Case 1:06-cr-00442-TCB-AJB   Document 209-1   Filed 03/07/16   Page 4 of 4

1   Mr. Watkins and Agent Brown's attention that there was a

2   fugitive who was currently wanted for aggravated assault and

3   kidnapping that Mr. Watkins knew that person was in the

4   Atlanta area and in fact knew precisely where he was and

5   provided information to Agent Brown and, again, based on that

6   information that fugitive was apprehended and prosecuted in

7   Fulton County.

8   He also essentially, I guess you could call it

9   making a referral. Your Honor. He got another individual to

10   contact Agent Brown and said that that's somebody that you

11   should talk to and that was a person that Mr. Watkins had

12   come into contact with in the penitentiary. That person

13   cooperated with Agent Brown, and based on that information

14   Agent Brown and others recovered a kilo of cocaine and

15   arrested and prosecuted six additional people in connection

16   with drug trafficking.

17   I know on the A.U.S.A. scale to some extent I'm

18   still a baby USA but I have been around at least almost

19   6 years now where this is getting to start to mean something

20   and in my experience with individuals who cooperate in drug

21   cases Mr. Watkins is off the chart. He is in a different

22   league. There's perhaps only one other person that I can

23   speak of that I have used or I've known of in our divisions in

24

25   (see original court transcript for the entire conversation)

Episode X

King Snitch of the South — Rule 35 Sentence Reduction Payoff

June 14, 2000, USMS transported me from the old APDC in downtown Atlanta where I had been housed since December of 1999 to Atlanta Federal Courthouse to finally be granted my Rule 35 Sentence Reduction as payment for all of the cooperation, snitching, that I had done over the previous four and a half years. Upon my arrival at the Atlanta Federal courthouse, I was escorted by two Deputy US Marshals to the US Marshal's intake and holding area where I was once again placed inside of a holding cell within that area to await my court proceeding. Called out to court, I was escorted by two in-house Deputy US Marshals up and into the Honorable Willis B. Hunt, Jr.'s courtroom where my Rule 35 Sentence Reduction Hearing got under way shortly thereafter. While making Judge Hunt aware of the nature of cooperation, I had obliged the government, Assistant U.S. Attorney Catherine O'Neal informed Judge Hunt of the fact that HIDTA TF Agents were very interested in continuing our cooperation relationship after my release. And by the way, I was really looking forward to that phase as a result of the arrest made on my family members.

Shortly after making that statement, Assistant U.S. Attorney Catherine O'Neal is quoted as saying,

> *"I know on the AUSA scale, to some extent, I'm still a baby AUSA, but I have been around at least almost six years now where this is getting to start to mean something, and in my experience with individuals who cooperate in drug cases, Mr. Watkins is off the charts. He is in a different league. There's perhaps only one other person that I can think of that I have used, or I've known of in our division in the last six years who has provided this type of consistent and quality cooperation."*

After hearing those words come out of the mouth of a Federal Prosecutor, I knew then and there that I had become the "Sammy the Bull" of Atlanta. King Snitch of The South! The last paragraph on page 9 of the transcript from that Rule 35 Sentence Reduction Hearing will substantiate Catherine O'Neal's claim. (Revisit Exhibit C-1, pg. 9, line 16-21) The result of my June 14, 2000 Rule 35 Sentence Reduction Hearing ended with Judge Hunt cutting 120 months (Ten years) off of the 17 years and 7 months Federal prison sentence that I had, leaving me with two years to serve.

At the conclusion of the Rule 35 Sentence Reduction Hearing, I was escorted by the same Marshals to the intake/holding area and placed into the same holding cell that I had previously occupied. And now, I had to wait to be transported back to the old APDC which occurred hours later. A person who has never been locked up literally has no idea how mentally tormenting it is to sit in a holding cell with nothing to do but look at the surrounding walls and think.

In a matter of weeks, I returned to USP-Terre Haute via FBP aircraft, but prior to my departure from the old APDC, I made my fourth and fifth sale of information using information furnished by external sources and FLEAs. The same system was used in both sales, and the proceeds that I earned for personal gain were used on clothing items and other needs in preparation of my release after my return to USP Terre Haute. Given that I was out to court on a "writ," contrary to being a new arrival, I only had to endure the required intake procedure of being strip-searched before being issued the return of my personal property held within the prison's property room. I was escorted by prison guards to the prison's SHU, where, for obvious reasons, I served out the remaining balance of my federal prison sentence confined to a "Protective Custody" cell, never returning to the general inmate population.

Episode XI

Freedom?

Revenge?

$$$ Confidential Informant $$$

Newports?

The Grand Illusionist!!!

Amphitheater?

Backdraft!

!!!

At the beginning of the summer months of 2002, I had served out the remainder of my reduced Federal prison sentence and was released to begin serving out my three years of Federal supervised release (probation). Within the first two months of my release, I had relapsed on crack cocaine which ultimately resulted in me being arrested again and in violation of my supervised release.

Three months after my release from Federal prison, I was arrested and charged with aggravated assault due to an incident involving my daughter's mother. That arrest occurred within Atlanta proper requiring me to be locked up in Fulton County Jail prior to and throughout trial, which also resulted in my Federal supervised release officer placing a Federal "Hold" on me.

About ten months after my arrest, I was acquitted at trial on the aggravated assault charge and released from the custody of the Fulton County Sheriff's Department and into the custody of the USMS to await a supervised release revocation hearing resulting in me serving several more months in Federal custody and Judge Hunt issuing an order dismissing the remainder of my supervised release after the completion of those months. October 2003, I was back on the streets of Atlanta, totally free.

Now totally free and in need of cash, I decided to take HIDTA Agents up on their offer to become a paid confidential informant. Several days after my October 2003 release from federal custody, I was at the Atlanta Headquarters of the HIDTA Task Force, not only signing up to become a paid confidential informant, but also plotting ways to carry out my revenge for the arrest of my family members. Within a matter of days after signing up to become a paid confidential informant, I was out making my first drug buy on behalf of the HIDTA TF Agents for an ounce of crack cocaine at a cost to me of $700.00, which prior to going out to make the buy, I overcharged them at a cost of $850. Do the math; I pocketed $150.00 before returning with the purchase.

Prior to leaving the Atlanta Headquarters of the HIDTA Task Force, I was thoroughly searched by agents, revealing a nearly empty pack of Newports and the amount of cash that I had within my pockets. Though I never smoked a cigarette a day in my life, I carried the virtually empty pack for the perfect plot. However, on several occasions while at HIDTA HQ, I did step outside and light up one to make it appear that I was a smoker.

Prior to leaving HQ to go out to make the drug buy, I was also provided a listening device so that the Task Force Agents could hear and record my conversation with the drug dealer. Knowing beforehand that I wouldn't be able to return in the presence of the agents with the additional $150.00, I placed it inside of the virtually empty pack of Newports, balled it up as though it were trash and discarded it only to return to retrieve it later that day. Once back in the presence of Task Force Agents, I handed over the purchased drugs and listening device. I was once again thoroughly searched, only turning up the cash amount of the previous search as planned, and the agents paid me cash for having completed the transaction.

In the weeks to follow, I made several successful drug buys for them, purchasing various quantities of crack rocks for varying cash value. But on one occasion, I purchased cocaine instead of crack cocaine, which pissed off the agents who wanted solely crack cocaine. During that time, those charged with cocaine drug charges included white defendants, who received no more than a warning or slap on the wrist from the court because of their skin color. So, you see, cocaine is a racist drug, just like crack. Therefore, those with cocaine drug charges received a much lesser federal prison sentence in comparison with the much higher federal prison sentences for those charged with possession of crack cocaine. Yeah, you guessed it; almost all crack charges reflected a very dark demographic — 95% black defendants. As such, the HIDTA TF Agents wanted me to make only crack cocaine purchases with a restriction not to exceed 4.5 ounces (oz.).

Since I was well connected and being that it was commonplace among the community for me to carry large sums of cash due to my armed robberies, I could have easily made regular cocaine purchases for the agents exceeding 4.5 oz. However, placing a crack cocaine order exceeding 4.5 oz. was far from commonplace for anybody. That foreign, illogical act would have immediately triggered drug dealers to become suspicious of my actions and intent. Where I'm from, it just doesn't make sense for someone to even want to purchase cocaine in crack form exceeding 4.5 oz. Hell, if you can purchase crack exceeding 4.5 oz., you should be able to purchase more than that in cocaine and know how to and prefer to transform your own cocaine into crack. So, buying crack cocaine in excess of 4.5 oz. was out of the question because it raises eyebrows of suspicion, you see.

Of course, with each drug buy of varying quantities, I received cash payments proportionately. And you can bet that I overcharged HIDTA TF agents on a quantity to cash ratio using the same extra cash modus operandi I had previously used, the empty Newport pack trick. I was never questioned about it. However, there was one question that a TF agent did ask me, albeit jokingly suggested that hit close to home.

Prior to leaving HIDTA HQ, on one of occasion, a HIDTA TF Agent commented, wondering if dealing with crack tempted me to relapse. After that seemingly sneaky suspicion, I started to wonder if it truly had become evident to them that I had in fact again fallen prey to crack. It was then and there that I had a heightened sense of the necessity of carrying out my revenge against the HIDTA TF Agents during my next drug buy before I became useless in my crack submissive state. My next and final drug buy for those HIDTA TF Agents consisted of me going to a car detail shop in Atlanta to make a purchase of 4.5 oz. of crack cocaine from the owner at a cost to me of $2,800 but $3,500 to the HIDTA Agents.

Due to several prior attempts to make purchases, the HIDTA Agents and I were both aware of the fact that there was a cocaine drought in Atlanta at the time. Therefore, the HIDTA Agents had no problem believing me when the drugs became available and I told them that the cost for the 4.5 oz. of crack cocaine had gone up to $3,500. Prior to leaving the HQ on my mission, I was thoroughly searched, revealing the cash on my person and the same Newports. Thereafter, I was given the $3,500 to make the purchase with both a listening and recording device contrary to prior operations with just a listening device.

After leaving the HIDTA HQ, an agent dropped me off as close to the car detail shop as possible without being compromised while other Task Force agents set up surveillance around the immediate and surrounding area. At the car detail shop, I was informed by an employee that the owner had yet to arrive but was on the way. Minutes later, the owner arrived in a gray pickup truck and instructed me to get into the passenger seat where I assumed the transaction would take place pronto. But the owner informed me that he did not have the drugs in his possession and that we had to drive to another location to conduct the transaction which, by the way, was perfectly fine by me. Prior to leaving the HQ that day, I had been instructed not to get into any vehicles to conduct the transaction and not to allow the transaction to be executed at any other location, because the HIDTA surveillance team would be setting up for that location only. However, when the shop's owner instructed me to get into the pickup truck and informed me that we had to drive to another location to conduct the transaction, for the following two reasons, I did just that.

One, I had no choice but to comply with the instructions of the owner, not if I wanted to get my revenge on them during this transaction. What was I to do, tell the shop's owner that the HIDTA TF Agents were surveillancing and needed us to stay put?

Two, I hadn't planned to bring the purchased drugs back to those HIDTA TF Agent muthafuckas in the first place. By the time that drug buy was to occur, I had already realized that I was too evasive for and could run circles around those agents.

To pull this off, I didn't need to become a magician, rather something much more sophisticated, an illusionist. The first illusion I created right in the listening purview surrounded by cameras and surveillance equipment was the appearance to my captive audience that I was actually inside of the car detail shop with music playing over the loudspeaker. Of course, in reality, I was outside the shop ready to make my escape. I guess I'll need to expose the secret of my brilliant illusion. Ok. So, hidden from the agents' view by another brand of truck identical in size and color to that of the truck that I knew beforehand the owner of the car detail shop would be driving, I had a plan. I placed the listening device on the ground next to the shop in a location where it was still picking up the music from the loudspeaker, of course, courtesy of the shop owner for the enjoyment of my Task Force friends, mesmerized at the "Car Shop Illusory Amphitheater."

The agents never saw me slide into the owner's getaway vehicle. Nor did they realize until much later that my presence was only a figment of their imagination, that I was not even in proximity of the surveillance arena. The illusion was performed masterfully, perfectly executed, my escape leaving them stunned, in awe and incredulous wonder. They heard the music, the fat lady sing, and I, the illusionist, received a Standing O! As in Oh my!...Tears and CHEERS or was it jeers? Yeah...JEERS!!

After perfectly executing my escape from the crew and discarding the recording device out of the passenger side window, I proceeded to go with the owner to the real deal location over in the Campbellton Road area of SW Atlanta to transact business for the pre ordered 4.5 oz. of crack cocaine. The transaction netted me the 4.5 oz. of crack cocaine and an additional $700.00. On the return trip, heading back in the direction of the crowd pleasing "Car Shop Illusory Amphitheater" but electing not to return to center stage, I requested that he drop me off at the Oakland City MARTA Station, nothing suspicious about that and still in the Campbellton Road area, where I transferred to a Transporter vehicle, familiarly referred to as an Ice-Age Uber, aka taxicab.

Once my co-illusionist was out of view, I quickly took up occupancy in one of two taxicabs idling and handed the Transporter two twenty-dollar bills and simply ordered him to just drive. Moments later, I provided him with an address. My first destination was a nearby family member's house where I secretly stashed 4 oz. of crack cocaine and $500.00 that I would double back and reclaim the following day. Prior to returning to the awaiting Transporter, I placed the remaining half ounce of crack cocaine inside of the Newport packaging to get high when I reached my next destination, not modus operandi. I went to a house located on the next street over behind the car detail shop which I had gone to earlier that day to make the drug buy for the clueless Agents. Once at that location, I quickly got comfortable and proceeded to smoke the half ounce of crack cocaine that I had in my possession. Retiring as an escape artist, for several hours, I smoked crack with the tenants of the house and other individuals coming in and out awaiting my frustrated friends at HIDTA. Look, I knew that one of three things would eventually transpire:

1. HIDTA TF Agents were coming after me with corrupt tactics, no doubt.
2. One of the crack heads that knew my location whom I smoked the half ounce of crack cocaine with would eventually "rat" or "snitch" out the snitch illusionist to the HIDTA Agents for little to nothing in return: just like a damn junkie.
3. Before that night was over, I would be arrested.

Between 10 and 11:30pm, all the above had occurred. Once 'crack-n-tell', aka 'crack intel,' smoked me out, the HIDTA Agents closed in on the location like firemen to a smoldering brush-fire, surrounded the house and then proceeded to make contact with the tenants of the house knocking with backdraft precaution in their wrists, calling out for a potentially violent or unrevealing response. The front door opens slowly, and there stands a woman with a backdraft of smoke and crackheads. The female was the head tenant and didn't seem too volatile, so the agents didn't feel as though they would set her ablaze by asking if she had seen me recently. She timidly stated that she hadn't seen me that night and further that it had been weeks since she last saw me — stated with questionable embers beneath the brush. Despite the smokescreen, the task force agents detected that she was smoldering with lies and asked to be granted access to the hot spot, then walked in cautiously when granted. There was literally nowhere to hide, but who's hiding anyway. My jig is up — retired.

You see, at no time during any of the events that occurred in daylight or moonlight was I not only on point and several steps ahead of the Task Force, but I was also prepared for the only type of outcome that could occur — me being arrested on a "Theft" charge. "So, come on in, arrest me, say helloooo to my little offend! Just a theft charge for the Grand Illusionist!"

However, prior to me being arrested, I didn't anticipate, nor was I prepared for what occurred the moment I was captured. Out of retaliation for my actions, the arresting HIDTA TF Agents informed all the occupants in that house that I had been snitching on and making drug buys from drug dealers in the Pittsburgh community for the agency. That — now that was the backdraft....and I knew that the aftermath would be singeing as it would become a wildfire as lighting a match against the HIDTA TF backfired and would not be easily contained amongst the drug dealers from Pitt.

They were pissed! But HIDTA TF Agents had no choice but to transport me to and book me into the Fulton County Jail on a simple theft charge. I was released from the Fulton County Jail the very next morning on a pretrial release signature bond (no cost to me). (Obtainable documents will confirm the entire theft incident and my involvement with the HIDTA TF Agents.)

Once released from the Fulton County Jail the following morning, I removed the $175.00 that I had concealed under the sole of my Nike sneakers and took the taxicab to my family member's house to retrieve the 4 oz. of crack cocaine and the $500.00 that I had secretly stashed there the day before. I instructed the driver of the idling taxicab to take me to a location over in the Pitt-area. It was time to party like the Crack Rock Star I had once again become as well as celebrate getting my revenge on those HIDTA TF Agents.

My coup de grace against the HIDTA TF Agents left them in a conundrum. They would need to account for the dud investigations and cases being built against targeted individuals that I had made drug buys from, all coming to a screeching halt...Scuurrrrrr! Yet, there was a kaboom! It all blew up in their faces: Time, money, equipment, manpower, all wasted. Less significant, though embarrassing, the agents had to account for the loss of $3,500 and the recording device. With that, the HIDTA TF Agents would be called on the carpet to explain to their supervisor(s) and others how they got outsmarted and played like fools by a Crack Rock Stud-_-well, Dud may be more appropriate.

As for the pending theft case, the court and I addressed that issue months later springing forward to Summer 2004 with the court proposing 18 months probation, but Fulton County Probation Department opposed. Apparently, in light of my extensive arrest record, Fulton County didn't feel as though I was a good candidate for probation, ultimately resulting in the court sentencing me to 18 months to be served in prison. I remained in the custody of the Georgia Department of Corrections until December 2005, only to find myself ten months later in Federal Custody on new charges and a rerun of cooperating with the government for nothing shy of personal gain.

PART 2 of 2

Episode XII

Crackhead Exposes Information Selling Scheme and Key Related Debriefs

In December 2005, I was released from the custody of Georgia Department of Corrections (GDC) back to the streets of Atlanta, I was a totally free man. And then, a rerun. But, unfortunately, not a sitcom. Within weeks of my freedom, I had once again relapsed on crack cocaine, and several months afterwards, I was back to committing armed robberies to support my crack addiction.

"I was back at it, crack addict, same facet, old habit."

On June 6, 2006, possession of a gun with an empty mag and high on a mixture of crack cocaine and ecstasy, I attempted to rob a grocery store located in SW Atlanta owned and operated by Koreans. To my dislike, I met face to face with Ms. Peppa Sprayed, introduced by Korean employees/store owners, sending me on a blind date. It was a hell of a date, my eyes burned of unspeakable passion. Instead of feeling as though on a date, it was more like inundated. She was into S&M and I was subjected to her sadistic aggression. I was restrained, subdued, deeply violated, and fell for my one true love: Ms. Arrestacuffs and Intake at the county jail. That arrested my passion.

Between the time of my 1995 armed robberies and that June 6, 2006 attempted armed robbery, I had committed over thirty-five successful armed robberies on a string of shops, restaurants, and grocery stores, purposefully and strategically, never once selecting a business owned and/or operated by Koreans. That mixture of drugs had clouded my judgment and altered my MO, fucked up my mojo.

Arrested by Atlanta's finest, I was charged with attempted armed robbery and illegal possession of a firearm before being transported to and booked in at Fulton County Jail. Within two-months, I was transported to Fulton County Superior courthouse in downtown Atlanta to attend a court hearing pertaining to my latest felony charges. It was at that one and only hearing that the charges against me were dead docketed (dismissed) at which time I learned from my court appointed attorney that the Feds were in the process of picking up the state charges against me and turning them into Federal charges, meaning that once the process was completed, I would be taken into Federal custody.

Within twenty-four hours after my return to Fulton County Jail, I had one of the in-house jail Deputy Sheriffs check the status of my charges. He informed me that my charges had been dead docketed, but he said nothing about a Federal "Hold" on me, which by the way, I anticipated that. I quickly made a move towards gaining my freedom before the Feds made their move.

Shortly after the status check, I made direct contact with the jail's in-house Deputy Sheriff Supervisor, Major F. Jackson, then proceeded to explain to her that all of my charges were dead docketed at court the day before. You think I said anything about the Feds? Hell to the no! Major F. Jackson was able to quickly verify the following: My charges had indeed been dead docketed, and I had no "Holds" on me. The end result of that verification by her was my release from Fulton County Jail hours later like clockwork at my cadence.

Two months after my June 6, 2006 arrest, and subsequent release, I found myself once again a free man, back on the streets of Atlanta shacking up with Ms. Crack Coca. My grandmother's house is my house and the only known and/or listed address for me, so I avoided laying up at home for obvious reasons. Sure, I was in love wit da Coca, but there were mitigating circumstances as to why I stayed away from home — My freedom was on borrowed time, but I had no money to flee Atlanta nor the Pitt community for that matter. Furthermore, I wasn't naive to the fact that eventually I would be captured. So, I spent my last month or so of freedom doing the following three things: Avoiding any and all contact with members of Law Enforcement, being as intimate with Ms. Coca as I could, and three, doing hella research and information gathering. I was preparing once again to meet my one and only true love, and we still gettin' it on right now, unfortunately — me and Ms. Arrestacuffs. Realizing my arrest was imminent, I was getting all my ducks in a row in preparation for my upcoming cooperation, eagerly anticipating what I do best in Prisonland, "Snitching for Personal Gain." It's sad to admit that besides taking the time to write this book, my only achievements in life have been the birth of my beautiful daughter and 'SNITCHING'.

Three days into October 2006, I made the mistake of going home to mow the lawn for my grandparents (whom I'd do anything for)—but man, the smell of fresh cut grass, it's irresistibly fragrant, you know. Federal ATF Agents pulled up in a van, quickly dismounting, violating my aroma therapy. But did I really make a mistake? I mean, hell, I was tired of running, and I knew this nirvana would soon end in being Taken III, IV, V...I don't know, I lost count. Just couldn't distinguish if it were nirvana or nerve-racking being free.

The Federal ATF Agents took me to an unfamiliar location for intake. I've become a professional detainee, posing for pictures and scanning my paws — it's all second nature now. Maybe I'm preparing for reincarnation, a male model in the afterlife. They transported me to APDC to be housed with numerous other federal detainees until December 2008.

Within twenty-four hours after my arrest, I was transported by APDC officers to the Atlanta Federal Courthouse for my first court appearance. Escorted to the US Marshal's intake and holding area, I was placed in the custody of USMS. At my scheduled court hearing, the charges against me were read aloud. I was denied bond and appointed a Federal Defender. I was once again being charged with interfering with interstate commerce and a 924(c), gun charge. However, my second 924(c) gun charge alone carried a mandatory minimum prison sentence of twenty-five years. I was then escorted by two in-house marshals and transported back to the APDC.

Several days after my first court appearance, I met my court appointed Federal Defender, Ms. Vionnette Reyes Johnson, for the first time. Observantly, I realized at that first encounter that my newly appointed Federal Defender was not the aggressive pit-bull that Mr. Kish was, regarding the quality of my legal representation. I already knew what I was up against, so I made it known to Ms. Johnson from the beginning that I would be taking the cooperation route. However, Ms. Johnson wanted to pursue a variety of other avenues of defense on my behalf in hopes of a favorable outcome. Therefore, for the nine months that followed, I allowed Ms. Johnson to pursue those avenues while I slept off my crack cocaine withdrawals, gained weight, and waited for my brain cells to realign and start functioning again.

For whatever reason, between that first meeting and July 27, 2007, the interference with interstate commerce charge was dropped, leaving me with only the 924(c) gun charge. By the time Ms. Johnson had exhausted all other avenues of defense, I was rejuvenated and had already gone to work on establishing my cooperation resulting in the scheduling of my first debriefing in regards to my second Fed-case (case no. 1:06-CR-442-TCB-AJB). It was scheduled for and conducted on July 27, 2007, the same day that I pled guilty, signing a 30-year plea agreement with the government, effective prison term contingent on the outcome of my cooperation. By now, you're aware that I was precisely in tune with the type and level of cooperation that would be required to reduce a 30-year sentence. So, let's do a slight rewind so that I can get to some of the details surrounding the plea.

On that day, my focus was both the debriefing and the plea agreement. I was taken to Atlanta Federal Courthouse for the debriefing, and you know what time it was...enduring the old routine. Hours later, I was called out of the holding cell to face my arresting Federal ATF Agent and a FLEA that I had been cooperating with years earlier before being escorted by the two federal agents to the Atl-USAO for my prearranged debriefing.

While en route, the Federal Agent, whom I had prior dealings with, informed me that he was there that day to make me feel comfortable but also to inform me that my arresting Federal ATF Agent too was a member of the inner circle. He clutched it for me by assuring that all the prior methods of operation were still in play and could and would be utilized throughout the course of my cooperation. (Obtainable legal documentation will confirm the presence of the Federal Agent that I had cooperated with throughout the course of my first Fed-case. In attendance at my first debriefing (7-27-07) pertaining to my second Federal case).

At the Atl-USAO, the escorts and I entered a conference room that was used to conduct the debriefing where others awaited our arrival. With introductions out of the way, the Federal Agent assigned to my first case quickly made the Assistant U.S. Attorney and others that were present aware of the quality of cooperation that I would be providing by confidently and boldly stating with a warm smile that I was Mr. Job Security.

Look, I had verbally agreed to a 30-year plea agreement prior to the scheduling at the start of that debriefing, and, later, I would sign it. That, I was sure of. Like a lion or tiger stalking the Serengeti or Zimbabwe plains, I was ready to pounce off the rip, clawing with razor sharp strokes of irresistible brow raising nuggets of information. Therefore, I came out swinging, slinging torn flesh with a 2004 murder within the Pittsburgh community, committed by one of its own drug dealers that I had made drug buys from for the HIDTA TF Agents. Actually, I had been the intended target of the murder and was on the scene, now an eyewitness. At the conclusion of that debriefing, I was escorted back to the US Marshal's intake and holding area, placed in their custody, then escorted by two marshals into the courtroom of Honorable Judge Julie E. Carnes, where I agreed to and signed the 30-year plea agreement and awaited transport back to APDC.

In 16 months, I participated in a total of ten debriefings, regarding criminal activity of numerous individuals and a variety of different issues, some conducted in the Atl-USAO and others within the APDC. Days after the conclusion of one particular debriefing and as part of my cooperation, I actually mailed marijuana to the Atl-USAO from within the APDC using the U.S. Postal Service. I was financially taking advantage of being housed with federal defendants that were fresh off the streets and having access to large sums of cash, and the corrections officers working the Federal Housing Units were doing the same. (Obtainable legal documents pertaining to Fed-case no.1:06-CR-442-TCB-AJB will confirm the mailing of the marijuana.)

During that 16-month time-frame, I also submitted several typed documents to members of the Atl-USAO pertaining to the criminal activity of certain individuals. (See exhibits D-1 and D-2). I had experienced basically every aspect of the Federal Court System while serving years of incarceration within the Federal Prison System involved in debriefings and otherwise instructing other defendants who sought my expertise on a variety of different topics of interests. It all came at a cost when it came to those individuals that not only needed my assistance in obtaining a 5k1.1 sentence reduction, but for those that could also pay the asking fee for my services. I made them aware early-on that there are three types of people serving time in the Federal Prison System:

Those that told,
Those that wish they had told, and
Those that wish they had something to tell.

A few of my clients were white, charged with white collar crimes. The corrections officers assigned to my housing unit could never figure out what those individuals and I had in common. Nor could they figure out why a few of the white detainees had all of a sudden taken a liking to me. Some of the correction officers would jokingly refer to me as being a corporate thug. One of the most important things that I taught was how to best utilize their accessible funds. Time and time again I've heard other individuals serving Federal Prison Sentences and even those not yet sentenced say that you can't buy your way out of federal custody because money is of no significance to the Feds, nor do the Feds care about how much money you have. My response to such a statement is, "Bullshiii—You show me a person sitting in Federal Prison or Federal Custody that has $10,000 or better that can be used to obtain his/her freedom which is not used in such a way outlined in my seminars, and I'll show you a fool."

The entire Federal Court System is corrupt. Furthermore, the system is designed with revolving doors so to speak for individuals to come through the front door only to leave out of the back door. By now, you should have realized that the government is the biggest buyer of information. Instead of paying in cash, the government pays in the form of sentence reductions. The Feds might talk that crap about not accepting third party cooperation and/or not accepting cooperation pertaining to individuals and subject matter that you don't have any firsthand knowledge of. But I'm here to tell you that that is a bold-faced **"Lie!"**

Before the end of this book I will make you aware of the existence of indisputable evidence, clearly proving that the Feds have not only had full knowledge of the buying and selling of information but indisputable evidence also proving that FLEAs have been authorizing, allowing, accepting, and approving the buying and selling of information.

Shortly after the beginning of 2008, I made several more sales of information, using information obtained from my external sources and information furnished to me by FLEAs. It is also during that time that I submitted the two typed documents consisting of viable criminal activity information offered as Exhibits D-1 and D-2 to the Atl-USAO.

Concerning my first sale in 2008, that was done using information that I had obtained from my external sources but also taking advantage of used information in which I myself had already submitted to the Atl-USAO (See Exhibit D-1). When approached by the buyer in that transaction, I had not yet received new information from my external sources, nor had I received any new information from federal agents. As the saying goes, "drastic times call for drastic measures," so, I had to improvise.

The end result of my first sale of 2008, not only resulted in the purchased information being used by federal agents in an affidavit submitted to a Federal Judge seeking approval for the use of a wiretap in regards to F-1 Court Case number 1:09-CR-482-TWT-LTW but also resulted in the buyer receiving the 5k1.1 sentence reduction that he had paid and hoped for, not to be confused with prayed and hoped for.

In regards to my second sale of 2008, I used information that was furnished to me by FLEAs pertaining to Defendant #1 in Fed-case number 1:09-CR-177-MEF-GGB. I had personal knowledge regarding Defendant #1. Upon receiving the updated information that I sold shortly after, I was instructed by the federal agents that had furnished me with the updated information to submit my personal knowledge of information pertaining to Defendant #1 directly to the Atl-USAO, which I did thereafter in the form of a typed-up document consisting of the information (Entered as Exhibit D-2).

Defendant #1 in Fed-case number 1:09-CR-177-MEF-GGB just so happens to be a well-loved and very close family member of celebrity Kandi Burruss, a member of the Atlanta based music group "Xscape." Kandi also starred on the popular television show, "Real Housewives of Atlanta." Not only is Defendant #1 currently sitting in a Federal Prison somewhere serving a Federal Prison sentence exceeding twenty years, but Kandi Burruss and her family members will likely have no idea at all until the publication of this book that their family member is a victim of the "information selling scheme" that federal agents and I were operating. (For end result see following Exhibit D-3.)

Had my 5k1.1 Sentence Reduction been secured prior to the debriefing that led to the selling of the information pertaining to Defendant #1, I would not have carried out the instructions of those federal agents, nor would I have been a participant in any way in the arrest, prosecution, and conviction of Defendant #1. My being put into that position of involvement changed the play of the game for me.

Exhibit D-3

Case 1:09-cr-00177-WSD-GGB   Document 277   Filed 05/25/11   Page 1 of 4

UNITED STATES DISTRICT COURT
NORTHERN DISTRICT OF GEORGIA
ATLANTA DIVISION

UNITED STATES OF AMERICA

-vs-

Case No. 1:09-cr-177-01-WSD

WILLIE MELVIN JONES

Defendant's Attorney:
Janice Singer-Capek

JUDGMENT IN A CRIMINAL CASE
(For Offenses Committed On or After November 1, 1987)

The defendant pleaded guilty to Count One of the Indictment.

Accordingly, the defendant is adjudged guilty of such count(s) which involves the following offense:

Title & Section	Nature of Offense	Count No.
21 U.S.C. §§ 846 and 841(b)(1)(a)(ii)	Conspiracy to Possess With the Intent to Distribute At Least Five Kilograms of Cocaine	1

The defendant is sentenced as provided in pages 2 through 4 of this judgment. The sentence is imposed pursuant to the Sentencing Reform Act of 1984.

It is ordered that the defendant shall pay the special assessment of $ 100.00 which shall be due immediately.

IT IS FURTHER ORDERED that the defendant shall notify the United States Attorney for this district within thirty days of any change of name, residence, or mailing address until all fines, restitution, costs and special assessments imposed by this judgment are fully paid.

Defendant's Soc. Sec. No.   XXX-XX-1966
Defendant's Date of Birth: 1966
Defendant's Mailing Address:
Atlanta, Georgia

Date of Imposition of Sentence:5/24/2011

Signed this the 25th day of May, 2011.

WILLIAM S. DUFFEY, JR.
UNITED STATES DISTRICT JUDGE

Case 1:09-cr-00177-WSD-GGB   Document 277   Filed 05/25/11   Page 3 of 4

1:09-cr-177-01-WSD : WILLIE MELVIN JONES
SUPERVISED RELEASE

Upon release from imprisonment, the defendant shall be on supervised release for a term of **ten (10) years.**

While on supervised release, the defendant shall not commit another federal, state or local crime and shall not illegally possess a controlled substance. The defendant shall comply with the standard and special conditions that have been adopted by this court (set forth below). If this judgment imposes a restitution obligation, it shall be a condition of supervised release that the defendant pay any such restitution that remains unpaid at the commencement of the term of supervised release. The defendant shall comply with the following additional conditions:

The defendant shall not own, possess or have under his control any firearm, dangerous weapon or other destructive device as those terms are defined in 18 U.S.C. § 921.

The defendant shall report in person to the probation office in the district to which the defendant is released within 72 hours of release from the custody of the Bureau of Prisons.

The defendant shall refrain from any unlawful use of a controlled substance. The defendant shall submit to one drug test within 15 days of placement on supervised release and at least two periodic drug tests thereafter as directed by the probation officer.

The defendant shall participate as directed in a program approved by the Probation Officer for treatment of narcotic addiction or drug or alcohol dependency which may include testing for the detection of substance use or abuse. Further, the defendant shall be required to contribute to the costs of services for such treatment not to exceed an amount determined reasonable by the Probation Officer based on ability to pay or availability of third party payment and in conformance with the Probation Office's Sliding Scale for Substance Abuse Treatment Services.

The defendant shall cooperate with DNA collection at the direction of the Probation Officer.

The defendant shall submit to a search and seizure of his person or property at the direction of the Probation Officer.

The defendant is denied federal benefits as described by 21 U.S.C. § 862(a)(1) for a period of up to ten years.

Case 1:09-cr-00177-WSD-GGB   Document 277   Filed 05/25/11   Page 4 of 4

1:09-cr-177-01-WSD : WILLIE MELVIN JONES
STANDARD CONDITIONS OF SUPERVISION

While the defendant is on supervised release pursuant to this judgment, the defendant shall not commit another federal, state or local crime. In addition:

1. The defendant shall not leave the judicial district without the permission of the court or probation officer;

2. The defendant shall report to the probation officer as directed by the court or probation officer and shall submit a truthful and complete written report within the first five days of each month;

3. The defendant shall answer truthfully all inquiries by the probation officer and follow the instructions of the probation officer;

4. The defendant shall support his or her dependents and meet other family responsibilities;

5. The defendant shall work regularly at a lawful occupation unless excused by the probation officer for schooling, training, or other acceptable reasons;

6. The defendant shall notify the probation officer within 72 hours of any change in residence or employment;

7. The defendant shall refrain from the excessive use of alcohol and shall not purchase, possess, use, distribute, or administer any narcotic or other controlled substance, or any paraphernalia related to such substances, except as prescribed by a physician, and shall submit to periodic urinalysis tests as directed by the probation officer to determine the use of any controlled substance;

8. The defendant shall not frequent places where controlled substances are illegally sold, used, distributed, or administered;

9. The defendant shall not associate with any persons engaged in criminal activity, and shall not associate with any person convicted of a felony unless granted permission to do so by the probation officer;

10. The defendant shall permit a probation officer to visit him or her at any time at home or elsewhere and shall permit confiscation of any contraband observed in plain view by the probation officer;

11. The defendant shall notify the probation officer within 72 hours of being arrested or questioned by a law enforcement officer;

12. The defendant shall not enter into any agreement to act as an informer or a special agent of a law enforcement agency without the permission of the court;

13. As directed by the probation officer, the defendant shall notify third parties of risks that may be occasioned by the defendant's criminal record or personal history or characteristics, and shall permit the probation officer to make such notifications and to confirm the defendant's compliance with such notification requirement.

Case 1:09-cr-00177-WSD-GGB   Document 277   Filed 05/25/11   Page 2 of 4

1:09-cr-177-01-WSD : WILLIE MELVIN JONES

IMPRISONMENT

The defendant is hereby committed to the custody of the United States Bureau of Prisons to be imprisoned for a term of **two hundred seventy (270) months**.

The Court recommends the defendant be incarcerated at FCI Jessup.

The defendant is remanded to the custody of the United States Marshal.

RETURN

I have executed this judgment as follows:

_____

_____

_____

_____

Defendant delivered on _____ to _____

at_____, with a certified copy of this judgment.

_____
UNITED STATES MARSHAL

By:_____
Deputy U.S. Marshal

Episode XIII

The Triple Cross — 5k1.1 – Rule 35 Sentence Reduction Leak

Months after my second sale of 2008, the Assistant U.S. Attorney assigned to my Fed-case and my arresting Federal ATF Agent informed me that as one of the requirements for the government filing a 5k1.1 Sentence Reduction motion on my behalf, my assistance would be required in "Stacking the Deck" in an upcoming Federal Trial. Whereas nothing beats the double cross except the triple cross, that's exactly what I did. Instead of assisting the Atl-USAO and FLEAs in "Stacking the Deck" in that up-coming federal trial, I sent out letters, characteristic of a whistle-blower, to the U.S. Department of Justice and to several news outlets reporting the illegal and corrupt activities of the Assistant U.S. Attorney assigned to my Fed-case who was immediately removed. The illegal and corrupt activities of my arresting Federal ATF Agent in documented records of my second Fed-case will confirm that I filed that complaint against the said individuals with an immediate investigation following. I have since been the subject of relentless vindictive retaliation from members of the Atl-USAO (my current incarceration for 13 straight years without being sentenced is one of them).

If by chance you are wondering the reasoning behind my decision to turn on the Atl-USAO, the answer is, a THIRTY-YEAR Plea Agreement. Whereas, I had agreed to it, I knew I needed to bring a shark to the party instead of a duck to reduce that plea significantly, and by exposing the level of corruption that I was exposing, I could do just that, if not completely.

It was during that same time period in 2008 that a federal detainee by the name of James Rochester would just so happen to stumble upon and learn about the elaborate scheme of "information selling." This was supposed to be held secret except for cooperating federal inmates ("The Small Fish") operating the scheme on behalf of all parties involved and federal agents and prosecutors ("The Big Fish") behind the scenes of the scheme.

Once a source beyond the circumference of the inner circle happens to somehow stumble upon and report these schemes, as a means of covering their tracks, federal agents present the appearance of innocence of knowledge of and/or involvement in the "Information Selling Scheme." That's where creative sanctions kick in. On several occasions, federal prosecutors in Atlanta went so far as to charge, prosecute, and convict the cooperating federal inmate(s). These are the inmates operating the "Information Selling Scheme." So, here's the creative twist. They convict only to turn around at a later date and reward the cooperating federal inmate with a 5k1.1 or rule 35 sentence reduction as payment for their participation in the "Information Selling Scheme." How do they sleep at night...slime...scum! Integrity? They spell integrity C-O-R-R-U-P-T-I-O-N (Revisit Exhibit B-2 and see Exhibit B-3) However, I have taken part in so much corrupt and illegal activity with federal agents and federal prosecutors in Atlanta for obvious reasons, clearly indicating and proving that any involvement in these "Information Selling Schemes" on my behalf was done at the consent and authorization of FLEAs and federal prosecutors. These federal prosecutors have never sought to charge, prosecute, or convict me for operating or being involved in any of the Reported "Information Selling Schemes."

They simply filed a 5k1.1 Sentence Reduction motion on behalf of federal defendant James Rochester, instructing FLEAs to not only cease all communication with me, but to also cease the acceptance of cooperation from me.

And as for their two reasons for refusing to file a 5k1.1 Sentence Reduction motion with the court on my behalf:

1. **They have repeatedly cited that my involvement in the "Information Selling Scheme" has put me in violation of the terms of my plea agreement with the government.**
2. **The other cited reason being that I haven't provided "Substantial Assistance" to the government which comes after an overall total of fifteen debriefings.**

Whaaaat??!! How do the amazing stats even allow them to form their mouths to utter such fabrication with a straight face? 15 briefings?!!!

Here you have federal prosecutors in Atlanta **honoring the plea agreement of "Gregory Harris" and others** after charging, prosecuting, and convicting those individuals of operating and being involved in the reported "Information Selling Schemes," while on the other hand, you have them **refusing to honor my plea agreement with the government for the same exact actions even though I have — Never Been Charged, Never Been Prosecuted, Never Convicted of such actions!** They are Unchecked, Loose Cannons with Technological Sophistication! Playing a god having the soul of Satan! (See following Exhibit B-3) By that point and time. I went from being the **"Sammy the Bull" of Atlanta to being Public Enemy #1.**

Exhibit B-3

ORIGINAL

IN THE UNITED STATES DISTRICT COURT

FOR THE NORTHERN DISTRICT OF GEORGIA

ATLANTA DIVISION

UNITED STATES OF AMERICA

GREGORY V. HARRIS

: CRIMINAL INDICTMENT

: NO. 1:90-CR-266-6-JOF

GOVERNMENT'S MOTION FOR REDUCTION OF DEFENDANT'S SENTENCE PURSUANT TO RULE 35

NOW COMES the United States of America, by and through Counsel, Richard H. Deane, Jr., United States Attorney, and Janis C. Gordon, Assistant United States Attorney, and respectfully moves that this Court grant to defendant a reduction of five months in his prison sentence, pursuant to Rule 35 (b) , and shows in support thereof :

1.   This motion is filed pursuant to Rule 35 (b) of the Federal Rules of Criminal Procedure.

2.   On July 12, 2000, defendant Was sentenced to a term of imprisonment for fifteen (15) months, for conspiring to obstruct justice.

3.   Defendant has cooperated with the Government since he has been sentenced. In particular, defendant provided detailed information about an individual who similarly attempted to obstruct justice in order to obtain a Rule 35 reduction, in a case which was prosecuted in Savannah. That information was forwarded to the U.S. Attorney's Office in Savannah, and the

86

Savannah target has been indicted and convicted for his role in that obstruction scheme. Additionally, defendant provided information indicating that another individual, prosecuted in this district, made up information and reported it to DEA. in an effort to fraudulently obtain a Rule 35 reduction in his sentence. On March 15, 2001, defendant made consensual tapes with that target, and has agreed to testify against that target, should an indictment be returned.

4.   Defendant cooperated with the Government as far back as 1993 but did not receive any reduction in his sentence for that cooperation, due to jurisdictional matters. A copy of the Government's motion to reduce sentence, which was filed on July 1, 1997, is attached hereto.

5.   Defendant's assistance, as outlined above, has been and will continue to be "substantial" under the standards of Rule 35.

WHEREFORE, based on the foregoing, the United States respectfully recommends that defendant receive a reduction of five months in his prison sentence, pursuant to Rule 35 (b) .

Respectfully submitted,

RICHARD H. DEANE, JR.

UNITED STATES ATTORNEY

JAMES C. GORDON   D STATES TT
ASSISTANT UNITED STATES ATTORNEY

Suite 1800
75 Spring St. SW
Atlanta, GA 30303
(404) 581-6244

IN THE UNITED STATES DISTRICT COURT
FOR THE NORTHERN DISTRICT OF GEORGIA

ATLANTA

DIVISION

UNITED STATES OF
AMERICA

:
:
:
:
: CRIMINAL ACTION
:

NO. 1:90-CR-266 GREGORY HARRIS

FILED IN CLERK'S OFFICE
U.S.D.C. - Atlanta

JUL 1 1997

LUTHER D. THOMAS, Clerk
By: _____ Deputy Clerk

MOTION TO REDUCE SENTENCE

Comes now the United States of America, by Kent B. Alexander, United States Attorney, and John S. Davis, Assistant United States Attorney for the Northern District of Georgia, and moves to reduce the sentence of defendant Gregory Harris, as follows:

The defendant was convicted in this cocaine conspiracy case on February 12, 1992, and was sentenced on May 8, 1992, to 292 months' imprisonment The court of appeals affirmed the conviction. United States v. Harris, 20 F.3d 445 (11th Cir. 1994).

The defendant, who began cooperating with the government beginning in about July 1993, has provided substantial assistance in the investigation and prosecution of other persons. Moreover, at least a portion of the defendant's assistance involved information and evidence not known by the defendant until more than one year after imposition of sentence. see Fed. R. crime P. 35 (b). Accordingly, the government hereby moves for a 33% reduction (98 months, with a resulting sentence of 194 months) in the defendant's sentence of imprisonment. The defendant's assistance is summarized below.

Beginning in July 1993, working primarily with DEA case agent Ron Geer, the defendant submitted to debriefings involving the

88

instant case, as well as a number of related drug cases. The defendant was interviewed by Al-ISA' s Buddy Parker, Jim Martin, and Candie Howard, and testified in several grand jury investigations , including those involving Thomas Pressley & Chad Clowers (see below) , Kenny Miles (see below) , Al Brown, and defendants involved in the Fred Tokars investigation.

. The defendant made several attempts to work proactively with DEA agents. In one instance, the defendant arranged for two of his associates to come to DEA to be debriefed and to cooperate with agents on the defendant's behalf. The two associates soon became unavailable and were later discovered to have turned against the defendant and to have informed other drug dealers that the defendant was cooperating with the government. The defendant s girlfriend also submitted to debriefings in an effort to assist the government. The defendant's girlfriend was contacted by DEA agents on two occasions but was not heard from again. DEA received information that the girlfriend had advised other drug dealers that the defendant was cooperating. These developments prevented the defendant from undertaking proactive cases for a time.

The defendant continued to seek ways to assist the government. The defendant referred Reginald Crawford, Germaine Powell, and Dennis Kens ley to DEA agents, who later debriefed them. The defendant also succeeded in encouraging inmates to contact DEA Agent Geer about cooperating with the government. Agent Geer referred inmates to the offices and agents responsible for their cases.

In June 1995 the defendant contacted Agent Geer about a firearms dealer who was selling illegal weapons. The defendant worked with ATF in an effort to set up a controlled buy of illegal weapons. ATF had previously been aware of the target and expressed an interest in pursuing an active investigation. The defendant spoke to ATF agents and made consensual calls from prison at their direction. Through no fault of the defendant, the case against the gun dealer did not materialize.

In July 1995, Kenneth Miles was arrested on a warrant from the Southern District of Georgia. Miles had been a drug target in this District since 1989. The defendant subsequently provided important grand jury testimony against Miles c and was a critical part of the effort to persuade Miles to cooperate with the government, and to enter a guilty plea in the Southern District and thereby avoid additional charges in this District. Miles has since testified in at least two federal cases and has been debriefed several times by agents in Atlanta and Savannah.

In September 1995, the defendant made consensual telephone calls to Tracy Little, a known drug dealer. The defendant made several calls to set up a potential transaction, and also introduced an undercover agent to Little over the telephone. A copy of Agent Geer' s DEA-6, prepared on March 11, 1996, and describing telephone calls made by the defendant to the Little organization, is Attachment to this Motion. A HIDTA task force agent was assigned to follow up on the calls and the investigation, but nothing was done until January 1996. In that month, Little was arrested in a "reverse" operation essentially identical to the one that the defendant had set up in September 1995. AUSA Catherine O ᵗ Neil prosecuted the case. The defendant was considered to be a key witness in the case against Little and his co—defendant, Demetrius Brownlee. The government used the defendant's debriefing for purposes of establishing drug quantities in the Little conspiracy; because of the defendant s statements, which corroborated those of another cooperating witness, the government was able to attribute a significant quantity of cocaine to Little. In addition, the undercover telephone call that the defendant made was part of the discovery in the case and may. have had some impact on the two defendants! eventual decisions to plead guilty. Little later cooperated with the government.

In December 1995. the defendant testified in a retrial in the Middle District of Georgia against Fredel Williamson, prosecuted by AUSA Mike Solis. The defendant ᴵs testimony against Williamson was accurate and credible; he said that he had obtained between five and eight kilograms of cocaine per week from Williamson, totaling 200 to 300 kilos. Kenny Miles also testified in the Williamson trial, and Williamson was convicted on all three counts.

In United States v. Thomas Pressley, a large cocaine conspiracy prosecuted in this District by AUSA Jim Martin, the defendant twice appeared as a witness. The defendant was debriefed on the, Pressley drug ring in October 1993, and, on May 4, 1994, the defendant testified before the grand jury. About a year later, Pressley and four other defendants (including Chad Clowers) were motion, consider all of the assistance provided by the defendant to the government, and not merely his assistance in the Little case.

Finally, because public knowledge of the defendant s cooperation with the government might pose a risk to the defendant, the United Court requests that this Motion, and any resulting action by the Court, be placed under seal.

WHEREFORE, the United States respectfully requests that this Honorable Court:

    (A)   Schedule a hearing on the instant motion;

    (B)   Upon hearing, order, pursuant to Rule 35 (b) of the Federal Rules of Criminal Procedure, that the defendant's sentence be reduced by 98 months, with a resulting final sentence of 194 months;

    (C)   Seal this Motion, and any action thereon by the Court; and

    (D)   Grant such further relief as is just.

Respectfully submitted,

KENT B. ALEXANDER
UNITED STATES ATTORNEY

JOHN S. DAVIS
ASSISTANT UNITED STATES ATTORNEY
UNI D S TES A TORNEY

1800 U.S.
Courthouse 75
Spring St.,SW
Atlanta, GA 30335

404/581-6017

Georgia Bar No. 211060

6

U.S. Department of Justice
Drug **Enforcement**Administration

REPORT OF INVESTIGATION			Page 1 of 3
1. PROGRAM CODE	2. CROSS RELATED FILES FILE	3. FILE NO. G3-%-0157	4. G-DEP IDENTIFIER HGCID
5 BY: S/A Ronald Geer AT: Atlanta, Ga.	G3-89-0035 ☐ ☐	S. FILE TITLE LI'ITLE, Tracy et. al.	
7. Closed Requested Action Completed Action Requested B :		8. DATE PREPARED March 11, 1996	
11.OTHER OFFICERS: S/A Charles Metzger, TFA Brian Anderson, NS SA Daniel Arrugeta			
12.REPORT RE: Conversations with Tracy LITIIE and acquisition of exhibits N23 and N24			

SYNOPSIS:

Attempts were made to contact Tracy LITTLE at his residence via the telephone in order to introduce an undercover agent to him. The undercover agent was to offer cocaine for sale. Several calls were monitored/recorded between Gregory HARRIS and Tracy LITTLE and others.

DETAILS:

4.   In September 1995, SA Geer received information from a confidential source (CS) concerning the drug trafficking activities of Tracy LITTLE and others. The CS advised that Greg HARRIS was attempting to contact T. LITTLE in an effort to introduce him to a source for cocaine. In late September, SA Geer began to monitor and record telephone calls between Gregory HARRIS and individuals at telephone number 404/349-7305.

5.   Intelligence information revealed that G. HARRIS had supplied T. LITIIE with cocaine during the late 1980's and into the early 1990's. HARRIS was a multi kilogram cocaine trafficker who moved up to 60 kilograms of cocaine a month. HARRIS was convicted under G3-89-0035 on conspiracy to distribute cocaine charges. HARRIS was sentenced to 24 years in federal prison and was designated to the Federal Correctional Facility in Jessup, Ga. The calls from G. HARRIS which were monitored and recorded by SA Geer were made from the FCI in Jessup, Ga.

6.   The following is a synopsis of calls made by G. HARRIS to 404/349-7305. The calls were monitored, recorded by SA Geer and subsequently processed as exhibit N-23:

    a)   9-28-95 / 1:10 pm

G. HARRIS called 404/349-7305 and spoke to a subject identified only as "DUKE. G. HARRIS was told that T. LITTLE had just left. DUKE told HARRIS that LITTLE was out on the street and that he would probably not be in for the rest of the day. HARRIS told DUKE that he would call back later in the day that he was going to have his man 'Carlos' contact T. LITTLE.

11. DISTRIBUTION: REGION DISTRICT Atlanta-DIG OTHER SARI DOE	12. SIGNATURE (Agent) S A Ronald Geer r 14. APPROVED (Name and Tide) GIS William D. Hudson III	13. DATE 3.14.96 15. DATE 3.14.96

DEA Form

1 990)   DEA se.8smvEC)   DRUG ENFORCEMENT ADMINISTRATION
                              t is the property of the Drug Enforcement Administration.   *Originatin*
                 THC   ontents may be disseminated outside the agency to which loaned.   reptt
                 is   Previous edition may be used.
            Noit— it me its 3

                        Attachment "A"

REPORT OF INVESTIGATION (Continuation	1. FILE NO. G3-96-0157	2. G-DEP IDENTIFIER HGCID
	3. FILE TITLE LITILE, Tracy et. al.	
4. Page 2 of 3		
5. PROGRAM CODE	S. DATE PREPARED March 11, 1996	

b)   9-28-95 / 1:23 pm

G. HARRIS called 404/349-7305 and spoke to DUKE   who advised that T. LITTLE had not returned home. A second subject by the name of 'BRADLEY' spoke   to HARRIS briefly. They discussed his living with T. LITILE, DUKE and a subject by the name of Dirk. The phone was returned to DUKE who told G. HARRIS that he spoke to T. LITILE and delivered G. HARRIS's message. DUKE and G. HARRIS discussed the availability of cocaine. DUKE mentioned that business was slow in Herndon Homes. During the conversation, G. HARRIS told DUKE that he wanted to introduce his man Carlos to T. LITTLE, G. HARRIS explained that Carlos was his source of supply. G. HARRIS told DUKE that he would call back tomorrow.

        c)   9-29-95 / 2:45 pm

G. HARRIS called 404/349-7305 and spoke to DUKE. G. HARRIS was told that T. IXITLE had left and was at Herndon

Homes, in the projects. told G. HARRIS that T. LITILE was expecting his call earlier in the day. DUKE stated that T. LITTLE was out "handling his business' and that he did not how when he was to return. G. HARRIS and DUKE had general conversation. DUKE told HARRIS that he was out trying to make a dollar. call was terminated with HARRIS telling DUKE that he would call T. LITTLE earlier the next day.

        d)   9-3W5 / 9:38 am

G. HARRIS   404/349-7305 and poke to Tracy 111TLE. HARRIS told T. ü'1T1.E that he was going to give his source of cocaine (Carlos) LITTLE's pager   HARRIS told LITTLE that he would have Carlos put in his (HARRIS's) code of #99. HARRIS stated that Carlos could beat the price LI'ITLE was currently paying for cocaine. T. LITI'LE and G. HARRIS briefly discussed general topics and T. LITTLE's business in Herndon Homes. T. LI'ITLE stated that he was doing okay   and that he was able to put a dollar in his pocket and pay his bills. HARRIS and LITTLE discussed other subjects who were known to be in the drug business, some of whom were in prison. LITII,E also mentioned the Atlanta Police corruption involving a police offer by the street name of Pac-man. HARRIS asked T. LITTLE to send him money to be put on his telephone account and that he would have Carlos call him on his pager.

4. The following is a synopsis of a conversation between INS SA Daniel Arrugeta and Tracy LITTLE concerning a meeting to discuss LITTLE purchasing a quantity of cocaine. The tape was processed as exhibit N-24.

      a)   10-495 / 10:22 am

At approximately 10:20 am, SA D. Arrugeta placed a call to pager number 404/341-0289 with a code of *99. This pager number was obtained from G HARRIS. Approximately 2 minutes later, a return call was placed to the Group 1 undercover telephone. A subject who identified himself as Tracy (LITIIE) was on the telephone. SA Arrugeta told T. LITII.E that was Greg's friend and that he was in town on business. SA Arrugeta stated that he understood tut T LITTLE may be interested in purchasing some "oil' (kilogram of cocaine.) SA Arrugeta asked T. LITTLE how much may be interested in. T. LITTLE stated that he would be interested in one half can of oil.

DEA SENSMVE

3

REPORT OF INVESTIGATION (Continuation)	1. FILE NO. G396-0157	2. G-DEP IDENTIFIER HGCID
	3. FILE TITLE LITTLE, Tracy et. al.	
4. Page 3 of 3		
5. PROGRAM CODE	e. DATE PREPARED March 11,	

When SA Arrugeta told T. LITTLE that thought bethought LITTLE going to obtain more than one half can of oil, T. LITTLE told SA Arrugeta that he would possibly be interested in more but that he would like to meet and talk first. T. LITTLE and SA Arrugeta made arrangements to meet 10-5-95 at 11:00 am on North Avenue in front of The Varsity. T. LITTLE described himself as being 6'4', 200 pounds and stated would be wearing army fatigues.

5.   On 10-5-95 agents responded to the area of The Varsity in preparation for the 11 am meeting between Tracy LITTLE and SA D. Arrugeta. Agents waited until after 12:00 noon with no sign of T. LI'ITLE. An attempt to contact T. LITI'LE vas made via telephone with negative results. The tape recorder malfunctioned during the call thus no recording was made. Information later received from a confidential source indicated that T. LITLE got involved in an unrelated errand and was unable to make the meeting with SA Arrugeta. TFA Brian Anderson was to make additional attempts to coordinate a meeting between SA Arrugeta and T. LI'ITLE.

CUSTODY OF EVIDENCE:

Exhibit N-23 is a cassette tape with telephone conversations recorded on 9-28-95, 9-29-95 and 9-3()-95 between Gregory HARRIS and other individuals at #404/349-7305. N-24 is a cassette tape of a conversation recorded on 104-95 between INS

SA D. Arrugeta and Tracy LI^{T}ITLE. N-23 and N-24 were maintained in the custody of SA Geer and subsequently processed as evidence under this file number. exhibits were released to the Atlanta D.O. Non-Drug Evidence Custodian.

NDEXD.IG SECTION:

3. HARRIS, Gregory   NADDIS #2256498
4. 11TILE, Tracy NADDIS #3010437

DEA arm

1990) - 60

DEA SENSMVE

DRUG ENFORCEMENT ADMINISTRATION

This report is the property of the Drug Enforcement Administration.
Neither it nor its contents may be disseminated outside the agency to which loaned.

3

Episode XIV

The Proof of Agent Corruption

In December of 2008, I was transferred from the APDC to South Fulton Municipal Regional Jail located in Union City, Georgia, where I was housed until October 2011. The Feds had a contract with that facility for the housing of federal detainees. Had I endured the inhumane living conditions of the South Fulton Municipal Regional Jail many years ago or during my first incarceration, I would never have reached the level of being a career criminal. My life of crime would have ended abruptly after that experience. Shortly after my October 2011 departure, federal inspectors closed the South Fulton Municipal Regional Jail. However, the span of that dreadful 34 months witnessed my continued selling of information furnished by external sources and FLEAs.

Regardless of the instructions given to them by the Atl-USAO, FLEAs continued to accept cooperation from me. The game had to go on with or without the approval and involvement of the Atl-USAO. One way or another, all parties involved greatly benefit from the buying and selling of information. Careers are built, prison sentences reduced, and an exchange of cash for valued information or substance swap hands. It's the American way. Furthermore, my beef wasn't actually with or directed at the FLEAs that I had been cooperating with, rather with the Atl-USAO for lying to me and trying to play me like an absentminded crackhead, instead of the valuable snitch I was.

Recorded phone call transcripts submitted to the courts as exhibits confirms that FLEAs did indeed disregard the instructions of the Atl-USAO to continue our successful modus operandi, but it all confirms that FLEAs have known all along about, allowed, and accepted the use of my external sources in the gathering and selling of information. (See following Exhibit C-2) It was also during that 34 months that all the following events occurred:

For the first time, I made sales of information to non-American born citizens. There

was a change in my legal representation due to a legal conflict. On July 13, 2009, my newly appointed attorney, Martin L. Cowen III filed a motion with the court on my behalf seeking to get the court to "enforce the Plea Agreement" that the government and I sealed. On January 29, 2010, the first of two Evidentiary Hearings pertaining to my Fed-case (case no. 1:06-CR-442-TCB-AJB) regarding the need for the court to "Enforce the Plea Agreement" was held.

The January 29, 2010 Evidentiary Hearing was held in the Honorable Judge Julie E. Carnes' courtroom, and it was at the start of that court proceeding that I first came face to face with the two Assistant U.S. Attorneys newly assigned to my Fed-case. It was then and there during that court proceeding that one of the newly assigned Assistant U.S. Attorneys openly admitted to Judge Carnes that FLEAs were fully aware of the fact that information was being bought and sold and that FLEAs were actually authorizing, allowing, and approving the buying and selling of information. Pages 114-117 of the transcript from that January 29, 2010 Evidentiary Hearing will substantiate the confession made by the Assistant U.S. Attorney and substantiate Judge Carnes' disbelief and anger after the confession was made. (See following Exhibit C-3) So, there you have it. I said to you earlier, before the end of this book I will make you aware of the existence of indisputable evidence, clearly proving the aforementioned. Whoomp, there it is! But wait, there's more to come! By the date of January 29, 2010. I had debriefed a total of thirteen times.

Exhibit C-2

Telephone calls to and from inmates are recorded. Counsel for Marcus Watkins requested a CD of these recordings for a certain period and discovered two calls between Marcus Watkins and FBI agent Eulis "Mile" Brosas.

File name: 9S0K10XG.v10

Start time: 9-28-2010; 02:45:39 p.m.

Length: 00:06:43

Mile Brosas' words are indented.

Marcus Watkins' words are flush left.

Hi, this is Mile.

Recorded announcement: "Global Tel Link. This call may be recorded or monitored. I have a collect call from [Marcus Watkins] an inmate at South Fulton Regional Jail. Press '9' for rate information. To accept dial '0' and hold. Thank you."

[Beep]

Hello?

Marcus!

Hey, how you doing Mile.

Good. How are you?

I'm alright. Did you finally get my letter?

You know, I just got back in town and I haven't seen it yet?

Awe, man!

Yeah, uh. I haven't had a chance to talk to the drug squad either, but... so

I got in touch with a FBI agent named Joe, he's working on somebody else's case, he connected me with a FBI agent his name Wasser?

Yeah, he's the acting supervisor on the drug squad right now.

Yeah. But see, this is the problem. I ran out of money on my phone. I was supposed to call him yesterday, which I tried to call him, to connect him up with my outside connection, they supposed to meet each other, got in touch with each other over the phone,

Okay

1

But I can't get in touch with him. Can't call his cell phone collect. Is there any way you can put me through to him or something?

> You know I don't think he is at his desk. I just saw him back in the back lot. I think he's out of the office right now.

Yeah, because [] I trying to connect waiting on me to give them the okay from them to get together, [] and my source outside. They going to plug in right in with the heroin connect.

> Hey Marcus is there any way that he can get a hold of you? Or do you just have to call?

Who Wasser?

> Yeah.

He can come see me. I don't care about dealing ... he don't have to go through my lawyer or nothing. I'm free to talk to anybody. If he can come out here... Let me tell you how we can do this ... but right now I am having phone problems because I don't have any money to get through. So if he can come out here he can sit in front of me and I can call my outside sources and talk to them and tell them that this is who I want you to deal with

> Right, right.

Source is not going to do something until he hears my voice.

> Yeah.

I can sit in front of yawl. I can make a call on your phone or Wasser's phone to my source and say, "listen, this guy, he's going to meet you whenever you guys decide to meet, whatever, and Wasser can take it from there.

> We'll let me. Getting a hold of him is going to be the tricky part. Let me try to get a hold of him and then let him know that he can come see you.

Tell him [] I can get all three of us on the phone, me and him and my outside connection and they can go ahead and take care of the business. I'll be out of the way. My cousin isn't going to do anything until he hears my voice with the agent.

> Yeah.

But let me tell you what the letter was talking about. I can't believe... I believe you. I just can't believe... There was a Federal trial that just take place three / four weeks ago. One of the juror members coerced some of the other juror members to vote not guilty. The plan was, even before the trial was started, before the not guilty, regardless of the evidence on this case. I'm going to tell you why the jury did that. The juror has a son that is a Federal inmate over at Lovejoy that's got pending charges and she's upset about the way the Government ... she feels the way the Government is doing [] so regardless of whatever the case was about [fall case?]. The US Attorney just lost a trial because they discussed the

2

case and everything [] even talked to the jury. So I didn't know what was going one. So they discussed the case during lunch and things and she told them [] she encouraged more jurors to vote not guilty.

Yeah. Yeah.

So it was a corrupt trial. The trial was lost even before the trial even started.

Let me see if I can't find that letter and pass it over to...

Let me give you the juror's name.

Okay.

You got a pencil and paper?

Yep.

Her name is Sylvia Madden.

Sylvia?

Sylvia is her first name.

Sylvia Madden?

Yeah. M A D D E N. She has a son that's a Federal inmate over at Lovejoy. His name is David Harvey.

H A R V E Y?

Yes. His name is David Harvey. He's over at Lovejoy with pending ... I think he has a gun charge or something like that.

Okay.

But she's the reason [] her and her influencing the other jury members to vote not guilty. I don't know how she did it, but she had already told me before the trial even started what she was going to do. She said she didn't give a damn whether the man was guilty or not.

How do you know her Marcus?

I met her through her son. She likes young guys. I see her. I was at my visitation and he was in my dorm and me and him used to shoot basketball and she's been trying to talk to me. She likes young guys. I'm not young. I'm 40 years old. But any way.

You're still young Marcus.

We've been talking on the phone [] relationship tips. But I don't have time for that. I'm facing too much time for a relationship. We talk on a regular basis. I can call her. Well she's at work right now. I can call

3

her anytime. And she told me. Discussed the case and everything. [] I don't know who handled the case or anything.

Yeah. Yeah. That's a good question. I don't know either. I'll try []

It shouldn't be too hard if you got the jurors name.

Right. Right.

You got her son's name. Maybe they can retry the case. I don't know. But I sent the information to Judge Carnes anyway. I sent you a letter with all the information. I sent Judge Carnes a letter with all the information. [] my situation with the US Attorney's office I've been just going routes to get my information turned in.

Okay. Well, let me see if I can't pass it along or find out more information about that. But in the meantime let me try to get a hold of Wasser and let him know. You're always welcome to call me and I'll try to find him. I'll try to give him a heads up that you're looking for him.

Tell him we can make a three-way call [] from there they can just meet each other around the corner [] my cousin can come to his office and they can just do whatever. I already gave him my cousin's name just that my cousin with the agent he's just not [] I tell him listen: the man is on the phone [] Wasser's on the phone. This is who you are going to be dealing with. Go ahead and introduce him to the heroin connection. He'll take it from there. They can go from there.

Yeah. Okay. Okay. I'll let him know then.

He can come see me tomorrow. Whenever he wants to see me. It's a hundred kilos of heroin and I need to make this happen. I got some ... he's got some other sources with some cocaine [] bringing a lot of cocaine to Atlanta. So you know it is what it is.

Okay. Alright.

Alright.

Alright.

I'll keep you in touch in case anything else comes along.

Alright. Thanks Marcus.

Okay.

4

Exhibit C-3

```
1                    IN THE UNITED STATES DISTRICT COURT

2                  FOR THE NORTHERN DISTRICT OF GEORGIA

3                            ATLANTA DIVISION

4    UNITED STATES OF AMERICA            )

5                                        )    NO. 1-06-CR-442-JEC-1

6              V.                        )

7                                        )    ATLANTA, GEORGIA

8    MARCUS WATKINS                      )    JANUARY 29, 2010

9    _____ )

10

11                       (TRANSCRIPT ORDERED SEALED)

12

13                       TRANSCRIPT OF PROCEEDINGS

14              BEFORE THE HONORABLE JULIE E. CARNES

15                   UNITED STATES DISTRICT JUDGE

16

17   APPEARANCES OF COUNSEL:

18   FOR THE UNITED STATES:        MARY JANE STEWART/SHANYA DINGLE

19

20   FOR THE DEFENDANT:            MARTIN L. COWEN III

21                                 DAVID A. RITCHIE

22                               OFFICIAL COURT REPORTER

23                                75 SPRING ST., S.W.

24                              ATLANTA, GEORGIA 30303

25                                   (404) 215-1516
```

UNITED STATES DISTRICT COURT

105

Case 1:06-cr-00442-TCB-AJB   Document 209-1   Filed 03/07/16   Page 3 of 7

```
 1                                          INDEX
 2    VIONNETTE REYES JOHNSON
 3          DIRECT BY MR. COWEN / CROSS BY MS. STEWART
 4    MARCUS ANTONIO WATKINS
 5          DIRECT BY MR. COWEN / CROSS BY MS. STEWART
 6    PETER C. BECK
 7          DIRECT BY MS. STEWART
 8    EULIS MILE BROSAS
 9          DIRECT BY MS. STEWART
10    BRENDA SUMMERS
11          DIRECT BY MS. STEWART
12
13
14
15
16
17
18
19
20
21
22
23
24
25
```

UNITED STATES DISTRICT COURT

1   MS. STEWART: SURE.   WE WOULD HATE FOR HER FAMILY TO

2   HATE TO WAIT.

3   YOUR HONOR, I'D LIKE TO PUT ON THE RECORD A

4   DISCLOUSURE THAT I MADE TO MR. COWEN OVER THE LUNCHEON HOUR.

5   IN LIGHT OF MR. SOME OF MR. WATKINS' TESTIMONY, I

6   KNOW OF A SITUATION THAT I FEEL LIKE I SHOULD DISCLOSE TO THE

7   COURT AND I HAVE ALREADY DISCLOSED TO MR. COWEN INVOLVING

8   MR. LUMSDEN, WHO HAD A PERSON COME TO ATLANTA TO COOPERATE ON

9   MR. LUMSDEN'S HALF.

10   THE COURT: IS IT LUNGSTON OR LUMSDEN

11   MS. STEWART: IT'S LUMSDEN, I THINK.

12   THE COURT: LUMSDEN?

13   MS. STEWART: L-U-M-S-D-E-N I THINK IS THE CORRECT SPELLING.

                     THE COURT: OKAY.

15   MS. STEWART: AND HE WAS COOPERATING WITH THE SECRET

16   SERVICE, I BELIEVE, AND MR. LUMSDEN WOULD GIVE MONEY TO THE

17   PERSON WHO WAS COOPERATING ON HIS BEHALF. AS I UNDERSTAND IT,

18   IT MAY HAVE BEEN MONEY FOR - - TO PAY HIS PHONE BILL WHEN THE

19   PHONE GOT CUT OFF BECAUSE THE AGENTS WANTED HIM TO HAVE ACCESS

20   TO A PHONE. HE MAY NOT HAVE HAD A PLACE TO LIVE AT SOME POINT,

21   AND AS I UNDERSTAND IT, MR. LUMSDEN MAY HAVE GIVEN HIM MONEY

22   FOR HOUSING.

23   THE LONG AND THE SHORT OF IT IS, I DON'T KNOW FOR OUR

24   PURPOSES THAT EXACTLY WHY HE GAVE IT TO HIM MATTERS. THE POINT

25   IS MR. LUMSDEN, AND SOMEBODY COME HERE WHO WAS COOPERATING ON

UNITED STATES DISTRICT COURT

107

Case 1:06-cr-00442-TCB-AJB   Document 209-1   Filed 03/07/16   Page 5 of 7

```
1    HIS BEHALF AND MR. LUMSDEN WAS GIVING HIM MONEY AND THE AGENTS

2    KNEW THAT.

3                    THE COURT:   OH, THE AGENTS KNEW THAT HE WAS GIVING

4    MONEY TO SOMEONE WHO WAS COOPERATING ON HIS BEHALF?

5                    MS. STEWART:   YES, YOUR HONOR.

6                    THE COURT:   HERE'S WHAT I DON'T UNDERSTAND AND

7    OBVIOUSLY THERE IS SOMETHING GOING ON THAT DOESN'T GO ON IN MY

8    COURT. THE GOVERNMENT IS ALLOWING PEOPLE WHO DON'T HAVE ANY

9    KNOWLEDGE OF A PARTICULAR CRIME TO GET THE CREDIT FOR THE

10   COOPERATION RENDERED BY A FAMILY MEMBER OR FRIEND ON THE

11   OUTSIDE. THESE WOULD BE PEOPLE IN JAIL. AND THEY ARE ALLOWING

12   THEM - - LIKE THE HESSIAN SOLDIERS IN THE REVOLUTIONARY WAR,

13   THEY ARE ALLOWING THIS TO HAPPEN?

14                   MS. STEWART:   I DESCRIBE THIS AS VICARIOUS

15   COOPERATION.

16                   THE COURT:   IS THIS HAPPENING A LOT?

17                   MS. STEWART:   I HOPE IT'S NOT HAPPENING A LOT, YOUR

18   HONOR, BECAUSE I KNOW AT LEAST INSTITUTIONALLY WE HAVE A

19   CONCERN ABOUT IT.

20                   THE COURT:   BUT APPARENTLY IT'S BEEN GOING ON WITH

21   AGENTS KNOWING. OBVIOUSLY I GUESS THE AGENT, IF SOMEBODY IS IN

22   JAIL AND IS TALKING ABOUT SOMETHING HAPPENING

23   CONTEMPORANEOUSLY, THE AGENT NECESSARILY KNOWS THAT SOMEBODY

24   ELSE IS GIVING THE INFORMATION.

25                   MS. STEWART: RIGHT. AND, YES, I THINK THAT'S JUST
```

UNITED STATES DISTRICT COURT

Case 1:06-cr-00442-TCB-AJB   Document 209-1   Filed 03/07/16   Page 6 of 7

1   THE WAY GENERAL INFORMATION OFTEN WORKS, LIKE MR. WATKINS WAS

2   SAYING HIMSELF, BUT WHEN YOU START TO PAY FOR INFORMATION, I

3   THINK THAT'S DIFFERENT.

4   THE COURT: IN YOUR CASE, IT WASN'T THE AGENTS GIVING

5   MONEY TO THE COOPERATOR, IT WAS THE DEFENDANT HIMSELF GIVING

6   THE COOPERATOR MONEY?

7   MS. STEWART: THAT'S MY UNDERSTANDING, YOUR HONOR.

8   THE COURT: BOY, THAT'S A BAD IDEA. AND WHAT AGENCY

9   WAS DOING THIS?

10   MS. STEWART: SECRET SERVICE.

11   AGENT BECK: THAT'S THE FBI, MARY JANE.

12   MS. STEWART: OH, FBI? I BEG YOUR PARDON. SO WHEN I

13   SAID SECRET SERVICE BEFORE, IT SHOULD HAVE BEEN FBI. I DIDN'T

14   KNOW.

15.   THE COURT: WELL, I MEAN I THINK MAYBE IN MY ALMOST

16   18 YEARS, THERE MAY HAVE BEEN A COUPLE OF TIMES I ACKNOWLEDGED

17   SOMETHING LIKE THIS, BUT I'VE PRETTY MUCH MADE IT CLEAR THIS IS

18   JUST BAD. AND, YOU KNOW, WHETHER OR NOT A DEFENDANT OUTRIGHT

19   TELLS AN AGENT I'M PAYING SOMEBODY THEY HAVE GOT TO KNOW THAT

20   THERE IS THE POTENTIAL FOR THIS TO HAPPEN, AND THEY HAVE GOT TO

21   KNOW THAT ALL THEY ARE DOING IS THEY MAY BE GETTING REAL GOOD

22   INFORMATION, THEY MAY BE GETTING PERJURED INFORMATION, BUT IT

23   IS AN ABOMINABLE SITUATION AND I AM REALLY APPALLED THAT IT IS

24   GOING ON TO THE LEVEL IT APPEARS TO BE GOING ON.

25   MS. STEWART: LIKE I SAID, BECAUSE I KNEW OF THAT

UNITED STATES DISTRICT COURT

Case 1:06-cr-00442-TCB-AJB   Document 209-1   Filed 03/07/16   Page 7 of 7

```
 1   PARTICULAR INSTANCE, I FELT IT NEEDED TO BE DISCLOSED TO THE

 2   DEFENSE AND TO THE COURT.

 3                   THE COURT:    ALL RIGHT. THANK YOU.

 4                   MR. COWEN:    JUDGE, I DO HAVE A CASE NUMBER ON

 5                   MR. LUMSDEN IF THAT HELPS IDENTIFY HIM

 6                   THE COURT:    ALL RIGHT.

 7                   MR. COWEN:    I'VE GOT AN INDICTMENT, KELLY LEON

 8   LUMSDEN, WITH 07-312

 9                   THE COURT: 07-312.

10                   MR. COWEN: THERE'S OTHER CASES, BUT THAT'S

11   SUFFICIENT TO IDENTIFY WHO IT IS.

12                   THE COURT:    RIGHT.

13                   MS. STEWART:    YOUR HONOR, JUST FOR THE RECORD THE

14   INFORMANT WAS NOT JUST PROVIDING INFORMATION BUT WAS

15   PROACTIVELY MAKING BUYS.

16                   THE COURT:    THE INFORMANT THAT WAS WORKING WITH

17   MR. LUMSDEN?

18                   MS. STEWART:    YES.

19   WE ARE READY TO CALL SPECIAL AGENT BECK, PLEASE, YOUR

20   HONOR.

21                   THE CLERK:    IF YOU'LL PLEASE RAISE YOUR RIGHT HAND.

22                                        - - -

23                                   PETER C. BECK,

24   CALLED AS A WITNESS ON BEHALF OF THE UNITED STATES, BEING FIRST

25   DULY SWORN, TESTIFIED AS FOLLOWS:
```

UNITED STATES DISTRICT COURT

Episode XV

USA TODAY'S Story, Not Mine — No Can Plea — A Painted Zebra is Still a Zebra

October 2011, I was transferred from the South Fulton Municipal Regional Jail to RADDF-Deyton where I'm still being housed as of the writing of this book and will remain housed until the outcome of my court proceedings which could be months or years from now. The Atl-USAO has retaliated against me since the publication of the USA Today article and my life has been in great jeopardy. It's sad to acknowledge I have been in Federal Custody for 13 years prior to the publication of this book, and still the ATL-USAO refuses to honor our agreement, but seemingly find pleasure in keeping me housed in the County Jail. This is Pre-Historic and still history in the making, but it is also cruel and unusual punishment. The courts have intentionally held up my Fed-case, not me. During this 13-year period, the Feds have had me just sitting "unsentenced" inside of several local jails and at the Detention Facility where I'm currently being housed. The RADDF-Deyton is a privately owned and operated GEO Corrections/GEO Group, Inc. (GEO) facility under contract with the government for the housing of Federal Detainees. It is a much cleaner and better overall facility than that of South Fulton Municipal Regional Jail. Upon my arrival at the RADDF-Deyton, I endured the, you know, all the normal intake procedures (Tuberculosis testing included) before being placed into the general population, A-5 detainee housing unit, several days later. Within a week after being placed in A-5 detainee housing unit, I had negotiated a $12,500 deal with a white detainee for the sale and purchase of some hot off the press information. I had originally met that white guy at the South Fulton Municipal Regional Jail months prior to his transfer to RADDF-Deyton. It took only a matter of minutes before he and I began to converse, which quickly veered toward the cooperation topic.

By that time, I had become aware of all the signs of cooperation and could smell the cooperation on an individual's breath just by talking to them. The deal between me and that guy contracted $7,500 up front and the remaining balance of $5,000 after the 5k1.1 sentence reduction had been secured. This guy got that $7,500 to my external sources so fast that I regretted not charging him more. I hadn't even obtained or delivered the information to him before the exchange of the $7,500. A review of my detainee account transactions will substantiate the increase of funds deposited to my detainee's account by my external sources during that time. The first deposit shows $600.00, and shortly after, $1,000 and so on. My assistance was so much appreciated that Mr. White Guy even had his mother depositing funds to my account!

The South Fulton Municipal Regional Jail and the APDC are nothing more than local jails under contract to house federal defendants/detainees FLEAs and I could maneuver better undetected. I realized that RADDF-Deyton was actually a federal facility housing only federal detainees better equipped with updated technology and monitoring systems which were going to make it harder, well basically impossible for federal agents and I to continue our modus operandi. Therefore, I had to rely mostly upon my external sources for information. I didn't make my next sale of information until July 2015.

December 14, 2012 is a date that I will always remember, a date that changed my life, forever. That's when my involvement with FLEAs and Federal Prosecutors in Atlanta was exposed to the world. How so, you say? USA Today, "MARCUS WATKINS – NOTORIOUS FEDS' SNITCH EXPOSED," front and center, mugshot and all, exposed as a government "snitch." If I had any ingenious gray matter before, on that day, it was all singed as this newspaper article burned through my frontal lobe straight through to my hypothalamus. The piercing punch from that article may have qualified as some variant of a careless lobotomy, but certainly a major concussion.

Although the journalist of that newspaper article made it appear that I had provided him with the contents of the information of that newspaper article, I did not give any form of consent nor did I have any involvement in its publication. Had I been the source, an active contributor to the journalist's news article, the July 26, 2013 letter sent to Judge Julie E. Carnes from the author of that newspaper article wouldn't have been necessary, seeking to get sealed documents pertaining to my Fed-case unsealed for the purpose of a second newspaper article when he could have come directly to me had I been his source. His request was denied. (See following Exhibit C-4) I never wanted my actions or involvement with FLEAs and Federal Prosecutors to ever be known and certainly not made public. NEVER!

On September 7, 2010, at the request of a federal defendant who had been one of several victims of my first sale of 2008 (case no. 1:09-CR-482-TWT-LTW), the court unsealed documents in my Fed-case for the review and use of the information contained in those documents by that defendant and his attorney. (See following Exhibit C-5) It just so happened that the defendant was being represented by the same attorney as James Rochester, the one that had learned about and reported the "Information Selling Scheme" that I was operating, and therefore, the attorney was knowledgeable of the scheme.

During that defendant's Fed-case, his attorney actually subpoenaed me to testify on his behalf during an evidentiary hearing in regard to the information that I had sold. Where I come from, self-preservation is the #1 law of the land. Furthermore, by testifying on his behalf, I incriminate myself, which definitely wasn't going to happen, and I would also be in violation of the signed plea agreement. Sworn in and seated, I pled the Fifth Amendment and was excused, leaving that defendant and his Attorney stunned and angry.

On that dreadful day of December 14, 2012, shortly after USA Today hit the hotels, newsstands, grocery and convenience stores nationwide, airports etc., I was promptly removed from the general population by members of the security staff, per the warden of RADDF-Deyton. I was then taken to a cell within the B-5 segregated housing unit and placed on "Involuntary Protective Custody" Housing status where I remained for 6 ½ years.

SOP for "Involuntary Protective Custody" housing status prohibited the housing of detainees in the same cell, so for the first thirteen months, I was in solitary "Involuntary Protective Custody" confinement. During that time, I had several unrelated quarrels with the Facility's warden, which ultimately led to a conspired physical assault on me that manifested on January 26, 2014 resulting in injuries which are documented. Several days prior to the assault, despite my protest and concern for my safety, the warden directed the placement of a hostile detainee in the cell with me. Only days later, he brutally assaulted me. I know what jailhouse lawyers are thinking right now, lawsuit.

I found out this detainee had been chosen specifically because of the high probability of an assault on me given that the warden was aware that the assailant had family ties to one of the many individuals that I had sold information on. He had openly revealed to others his dislike for me and his intent to inflict injurious bodily harm on me.

Jailhouse lawyers, speak up: circumstantial evidence? Since that assault occurred, there hasn't even been an attempt by the facility's staff to place another detainee inside of the cell with me. So the assault and "documented" injury actually occurred, and jailhouse lawyers say: non-frivolous lawsuit that will stick. Au contraire, to cover up that conspired assault and shield the facility from negligence, the on-duty Security Staff Supervisor, Lieutenant Ezekiel Cooper went so far as knowingly, willingly, and purposefully filing a fraudulent incident report regarding the January 26, 2014 assault. But the Lt. also knowingly, willingly, and purposefully withheld critical information/evidence from his incident report.

In his filed incident report, he did not record anything about the loose razor blade (contraband) that was used on me during the assault. The blade was found and confiscated as evidence along with several other razors (contraband) found in my attacker's possession by Lieutenant Ezekiel Cooper, himself, but also the Security Staff member, Bernard Dickens. Dirty bastards! Furthermore, because of the backing of the facility's warden, my attacker did not receive any form of disciplinary write up or disciplinary restrictions, whereas I, the victim in solitary confinement, did receive a disciplinary write up for being assaulted and disciplinary restrictions. (See the following Exhibit C-6 for Lieutenant Ezekiel Cooper's fraudulent Incident Report) Over my many years of incarceration, there's something that I've learned about privately owned and operated correctional facilities; It's all about business. The owners and stockholders all have a vested interest in the "high fill rate" of inmates to capacity. Prison systems are big business. The higher the fill rate, the higher return on their investment. Inmates are nothing more than property, a vehicle to net the highest profit. Because of this vested financial interest, the investors need, even if they don't want, convictions that are a bi-product or final product of arrests and long-term incarcerations. And I learned that most, if not all, supervisors and company administration of the facility have a by all means necessary demeanor to shield and protect the privately owned and operated correctional facility from negligence.

I filed a civil suit regarding the January 26, 2014 assault, which was dismissed due to improper service and circumstances beyond my control. I know. I've got your tickers up now — improper service — hmm. Shortly after filing the civil suit, the facility's warden was transferred to another facility in another state.

On July 18, 2013 there was another change of legal representation in my Fed-case. From that date forth, I've been represented by Attorney William A. Morrison. During that time and as a result of the USA Today Newspaper article, my Fed-case had gained a lot of publicity making the Atl-USAO very uncomfortable and desperately seeking a resolution in the case. In other words, the Atl-USAO wanted my Fed-case to go away. Release Me!

Within the first six months of representation, my newly appointed attorney presented me with a second plea agreement, submitted to him by the Atl-USAO favorable to that office. He spent several days, immediately following, trying to convince me to agree to the newly submitted plea agreement. No Sir! You've lost yo damn mind! I repeatedly rejected the plea agreement. Had I agreed to that second plea agreement instead of writing this book from a Federal Detention Facility, I would be writing it from a Federal Prison somewhere while serving that 30-year prison sentence. The only difference between the first and second plea agreement was the fancy wording and the Atl-USAO's desire to get me to drop my claim of vindictive prosecution as well as other claims against the Atl-USAO. After you get past all that, the second plea agreement would have rendered all of my cooperation worthless and would have still sent me to Federal Prison for THIRTY YEARS! HELL NO! I've given up too much valuable information to surrender it for nothing. I snitch for personal gain, not the moral ethics of a vigilante.

Concernedly, because my newly court appointed attorney tried to get me to agree to that second plea agreement within the first six months of representation for a slow-go Fed-case pending an outcome for six and a half years, I became very skeptical of the quality of the legal representation that I was and would be receiving from him. However, I was already six and a half years in and knew I had to play the hand that I was dealt.

In later months and years, I came to realize and fully appreciate the high quality of legal representation that Attorney William A. Morrison was and still is providing me with as of writing of this book. That said, I still can't account for his ushering me to take the disguised plea. That zebra was still a zebra, no matter how it was painted, but the best I can do is state that he felt at the time that it was the only offer on the table given that furor and strict latitude of ATL-USAO. I have forgiven him for that attempt, and I was smart enough not to go for it. I would also refer others, including family members, in need of a very good attorney, to Attorney William A. Morrison of the Morrison Firm phone number 470-444-9533 or 470-444-9530.

Whereas, I have witnessed and been a part of so much high-level corruption and illegal activity in regards to the Atlanta Federal Court System, I prematurely and wrongfully assumed that Attorney Morrison was working on behalf of the Atl-USAO and was a participant in such corrupt and illegal activity on a mission to sell me out. I now realize that I couldn't have asked for better legal representation. Jailhouse lawyers and readers, you still have a question that I have not answered, and I promise, I will get to that...lawsuit/improper service.

On May 13, 2014, I was debriefed for the fourteenth time. Which not only came after USA Today put me on blast, but which also came after the Atl-USAO repeatedly cited that my cooperation hadn't risen to the level of substantial assistance.

Exhibit C-4

Snitching for Personal Gain:

USA TODAY
A GANNETT COMPANY

July 26, 2013

VIA FIRST-CLASS MAIL

Honorable Julie E. Carnes
Chief Judge
United States District Court
2167 Richard B. Russell Federal Building
75 Spring Street, S.W.
Atlanta, Georgia 30303-3309

      Re: Sealed records in *United States v. Watkins*, No. 06-cr-442

Dear Judge Carnes:

I write to request that the Court unseal filings related to Mr. Watkins' motion to enforce the terms of his plea agreement.

As you may be aware, Mr. Watkins' case has generated significant public interest, in no small part because of the allegations that he operated an information-for-sale enterprise out of the Atlanta's jail. USA TODAY has covered that scheme, as have others. *See* Brad Heath, *Federal prisoners use snitching for personal gain*, USA TODAY, Dec. 14, 2012 at A1, available from http://usat.ly/UfYK7d (last visited July 26, 2013); Kevin Rowson, *Inmates are paying for information to reduce sentences*, 11alive.com, Dec. 14, 2012, available from http://on.11alive.com/XltVhS (last visited July 26, 2013).

Mr. Watkins' motion has now been pending for more than four years. Many of the records related to it remain under seal. In my view, continued secrecy is incompatible with the requirements of the First Amendment.

The press and public have long enjoyed a right of access to court proceedings and records, rooted in both the common law and the First Amendment. *Nixon v. Warner Comm'ns, Inc.*, 435 U.S. 589, 597 (1978) ("It is clear that the courts of this country

116

2

recognize a general right to inspect and copy public records and documents, including judicial records and documents."); *Richmond Newspapers, Inc. v. Virginia*, 448 U.S. 555, 580 (1980) ("[T]he right to attend criminal trials is implicit in the guarantees of the First Amendment."). This right extends to records filed in connection with criminal proceedings, *e.g.*, *Globe Newspaper Co. v. Pokaski*, 868 F.2d 497, 502 (1st Cir. 1989) (finding a "First Amendment right of access to records submitted in connection with criminal proceedings"); *In re New York Times Co.*, 828 F.2d 110, 114 (2d Cir. 1987), and to matters affecting sentencing, *see In re Washington Post Co.*, 807 F.2d 383, 389-90 (4th Cir. 1986). The First Amendment right of access is so fundamental that it permits sealed criminal proceedings only when secrecy is "necessitated by a compelling governmental interest, and is narrowly tailored to serve that interest." *Chicago Tribune Co. v. Bridgestone/Firestone, Inc.*, 263 F.3d 1304, 1310 (11th Cir. 2001) (quoting *Globe Newspaper Co. v. Superior Court of the County of Norfolk*, 457 U.S. 596, 603 (1982)).

This Court noted in a February 2, 2012 order that it "is uncertain that these documents need to be sealed," and indicated that "[a]fter review, the Court may unseal these documents." I ask that the Court revisit this question.

There has been no public demonstration of a compelling interest in keeping these filings under seal. (That interest cannot be Mr. Watkins' interest in concealing the fact of his extensive cooperation with the government, which he has already revealed to the press.) Nor has there been a public determination that maintaining the records under seal is the least restrictive alternative for furthering that compelling interest, whatever it may be. For example, the Court could instruct the parties to file redacted copies of the records.

Should you have any questions, please do not hesitate to contact me. I may be reached at (202) 527-9709, or by electronic mail at bheath@usatoday.com.

Thank you for your kind attention to this request.

Sincerely,

Brad Heath

Exhibit C-5

IN THE UNITED STATES DISTRICT COURT
FOR THE NORTHERN DISTRICT OF GEORGIA

ATLANTA DIVISION

UNITED STATES OF AMERICA   )
)
      v.   )
)   1:06-CR-442-01 (JEC) (LTW)
)
MARCUS WATKINS   )
)

**ORDER TO
UNSEAL DOCUMENTS**

Upon request of IVEY GRANT, a defendant in case number 1:09CR 482,

and with the CONSENT and agreement of the United States, it is HEREBY

ORDERED that the exhibits[1] and hearing transcript which were sealed on January

29, 2010, [*see* Doc. number 101], BE UNSEALED. The exhibits referenced in

Doc. No. 101, shall be unsealed and true and accurate copies provided by the

government to counsel for Mr. Grant, L. BURTON FINLAYSON, for use in the

litigation of 1:09 CR 482. Furthermore, the hearing transcript shall be unsealed

---

[1]Including Defendant's exhibits 1-3, and Government's exhibits 5 and 7.

and counsel for Mr. Grant may order and obtain a copy of said transcript for use in

the litigation of 1:09 CR 482.

SO ORDERED, this ___7___ day of September, 2010.

Julie E. Carnes
United States District Court Judge
Northern District of Georgia

Presented by:
L. Burton Finlayson
Attorney for Ivey Grant, 1:09 CR 482
931 Ponce de Leon Avenue, NE
Atlanta, Georgia 30306
(404) 872-0560

Consented to by: Kurt Erskine
AUSA
600 U.S. Courthouse
75 Spring Street
Atlanta, GA 30303
(404) 581-6000

2

Exhibit C-6

GEO SERIOUS INCIDENT REPORT 14-008

Incident Date / Time:	1/26/2014 7:40:00AM
Facility:	Robert A. Deyton Detention Facility
	11866 Hastings Bridge Road
	LoveJoy GA
Facility Location:	Housing Unit
Parent Incident:	
Region:	Eastern Region
Referral Authority:	
Incident number:	142601091895

Law Enforcement Notified:	Yes
Local Notified:	No
State Notified:	No
Federal Notified:	Yes

Incident Types

ASSAULT - INMATE ON INMATE ASSAULT WITHOUT SERIOUS INJURY C2

Number of Staff Involved: 4

Staff

Ezekiel Cooper, Supv, Shift (M)
Bernard Dickens, Correctional Officer (M)
Sidney Holston, Correctional Officer (M)
Ben Johnson, Correctional Officer (M)

Number of Subjects Involved: 0

Subject	ID	Sex	DOB	Arrival Date	Comment
Demetrius Pullins	46899019	M	07/18/1973	11/15/2013	Resident

Resolution Comments

Marcus Watkins	4640019	M	04/06/1971	03/21/2013	Resident

Resolution Comments

Incident Description:

On Sunday, 1/26/2014 at 07:40AM in location: Special Management Unit, B-5-203, Correctional Officer John Forth call for assistance. Upon arriving to the cell both detainees were engaged in a physical altercation. Detainee Pullins,Demetrius # 46899019 and Detainee Watkins,Marcus #46440019 were fighting inside their cell #203 in B-5.

Immediate Action Taken:

Lieutenant Cooper, Correctional Officers John Forth, Bernard Dickens and Ben Johnson gave verbal commands and both detainees to stop fighting to which they complied. Detainee Pullins was given a command to come to the handcuffing port to be restrained to which he complied. Detainee Watkins, Marcus was given an order to turn and face the wall, as Pullins was being brought out of the cell. Pullins was then commanded to come to the hand cuffing port to be restrained to which he complied. Both detainees were escorted to health services where an evaluation was conducted by Nurse Carr RN. Medical staff who noted the following injuries Watkins: swollen eye, scratch on the back and left shoulder and a cut to the right thumb. Detainee Pullins,Demetrius was escorted to medical and was seen by Nurse Carr who noted: right hand swollen near knuckles. Both detainees were cleared and returned to the special management and have been issued additional charges for fighting. Reportedly this fight occurred as a result of Detainee Pullins caught Detainee Watkins going through his personal papers and legal documents. Detainee Watkins stated he was jumped on because he was writing a letter at the desk that they share in the cell where Pullins had his mail.

Restraints Used:

Restraint	Comment

OPR Referral:	No
Worker's Comp. Ref.:	No
Client Notified:	Yes 1/26/2014 10:40:00AM
Person(s) Notified:	Chief H. Walker III GEO, AW D. Horton GEO, Warden R. Cherry GEO, Director K. Cauley GEO, ADO R. Becker GEO, ADO M. Heffron GEO, COR M. Moschetta USMS

Page 1 of 2

Episode XVI

Perjury Smudgery — Who Cares — Apparently not Government

Since Judge Carnes never issued a ruling regarding my January 29, 2010 Evidentiary Hearing, a second Evidentiary Hearing was in order. On July 29, 2014 the second of two Evidentiary Hearings pertaining to Fed-case number 1:06-CR-442-TCB-AJB and regarding the need for the court to "enforce the plea agreement" was held in the courtroom of the Honorable Judge Linda T. Walker. The first government witness called to testify against me was federal inmate David Joe Harvey whom I had sold information to while at South Fulton Municipal Regional Jail. Harvey is the defendant in Fed-case number 1:09-CR-148-AT-GGB. (See following Exhibit D-4) Shortly after the publication of the USA Today faux pas, Harvey had his court appointed Attorney contact and inform the Atl-USAO that I had also sold information to him while co-housed at the South Fulton Municipal Regional Jail in 2009, which occurred after the 2008 date that James Rochester learned of and reported the "Information Selling Scheme," clearly proving that my "Information Selling Operation" was ongoing without the consent and knowledge of the Atl-USAO. (See following Exhibit D-5) When negotiating the deal for the sale and purchase of information. For some strange reason I just didn't feel comfortable doing business with David Joe Harvey and should have followed my first instinct.

A tadpole will eventually leap into a frog. A maggot morphs into a fly, a caterpillar cocoons into a butterfly, but a snake... that's all it will ever be, a cold-blooded slithering snake. And like a moth to a flame, burned by the fire, I went against my first mind. Greed often blinds the clairvoyant!

I should have seen it coming a mile away, for Harvey had a slithering track record, documented history of lying to FLEAs and Federal Prosecutors admittedly during court proceedings on numerous occasions to get a 5k1.1 sentence reduction. I knew prior to his perjured testimony that the Atl-USAO was using Harvey as a government witness during the July 29, 2014 Evidentiary Hearing for the purpose of affording him the opportunity to do what he does best, tell a good lie. (See following Exhibit D-6)

In an effort to help her son obtain his 5k1.1 sentence reduction, the second government witness called to testify against me at my July 29, 2014 Evidentiary Hearing, was Sylvia Madden, Harvey's mother. (See following Exhibit D-4). He had turned the game of snitching into a family affair. Unbeknownst to inmate Harvey and his mother, I had previously (four years earlier/9/28/2010) provided information to FBI Agent Eulis Mile Brosas over the telephone regarding inmate Harvey's mother committing the crime of jury tampering in a Fed-case in which she was a juror. (Revisit Exhibit C-2)

However, being that I had become the Atl-AUSO's Public Enemy #1, those at the Atl-USAO didn't care about the Fed-case that they lost as a result of Sylvia Madden's jury tampering which also occurred while her son was in Federal Custody. All they cared about and still care about is getting their revenge against me.

Now, to pack another serious blow to the gut of the slime that these pigs wallow in, I promised more indisputable evidence, and this is Part II. You need look no further than the Fed-case United States v. David Joe Harvey (case no.1:09-CR-148-AT-GGB) for indisputable evidence proving that Federal Prosecutors in Atlanta have a long history and very common practice of knowingly, willingly, and purposefully allowing cooperating federal inmates (Government Witnesses) to commit the crime of "Perjury" on behalf of the government during the court testimony. Congruently, they have a patterned history and common practice of rewarding cooperating federal inmates with a 5k1.1 or Rule 35 Sentence Reduction as payment for committing the crime of perjury on behalf of the government then procedurally asking the courts to "Seal" the sentencing transcripts of those cooperating federal inmates as a means of concealing the facts from the American Public.

Instead of David Joe Harvey receiving his 5k1.1 Sentence Reduction based on information that he purchased from me, he received his 5k1.1 Sentence Reduction based on his testimony against me. The Atl-USAO was now using some of the same corrupt tactics against me that for years I had been the very perpetrator of. Subsequent to federal inmate Harvey committing the crime of perjury on behalf of the government, my Attorney and I immediately submitted indisputable evidence to the court (direct evidence, court filings, and contents included court motions), clearly proving to the court that the testimony that David Joe Harvey provided on behalf of the government on July 29, 2014 was perjured testimony. The submitted evidence also clearly proved that Federal Prosecutors in Atlanta did knowingly, willingly, and purposefully allow federal inmate David Joe Harvey to commit the crime of perjury on that date.

Immediately thereafter, I filed a complaint with the State Bar of Georgia against both federal prosecutors assigned to my Fed-case.

Exhibit D-4

IN THE UNITED STATES DISTRICT COURT
FOR THE NORTHERN DISTRICT OF GEORGIA

ATLANTA DIVISION

UNITED STATES OF AMERICA,	).	
Plaintiff,	)	DOCKET NUMBER
v.	)	NO. 1-06-CR-442-JEC
MARCUS WATKINS,	)	ATLANTA, GEORGIA
Defendant,.	)	JANUARY 29, 201
_____	)	

TRANSCRIPT OF MAGISTRATE PROCEEDINGS

THE HONORABLE LINDA T. WALKER

UNITED STATES MAGISTRATE JUDGE

APPEARANCES:

FOR THE PLAINTIFF: SHANYAES & MARY JANE STEWART

UNITED STATES ATTORNEY'S OFFICE

ATLANTA, GEORGIA 30303

FOR THE DEFENDANT:.   WILLIAM MORRISON

JONES, MORRISON, AND WOMACK, PC

ATLANTA, GEORGIA 30343

MECHANICAL STENOGRAPH OF PROCEEDINGS

AND COMPUTER-AIDED TRANSCRIPT PRODUCED BY

OFFICIAL COURT REPORTER:

MONTRELL VANN, RPR, RMR, CRR

1794 UNITED STATES COURTHOUSE

75 SPRING STREET, SW, ATLANTA, GA 30303

(404)215-1594

Exhibit D-5

Watkins Timeline

June 15, 1998
Watkins receives a Rule 35(b) reduction in Case No. 1:96-CR-032 for reporting an info-selling scheme to the USAO.

Oct. 24, 2006
Watkins is indicted in Case No. 1:06-CR-442

July 27, 2007
Guilty Plea (Watkins' agreement includes conditional 5K)

Aug. 21, 2008
USAO learns of Watkins' info-selling scheme from defendant James Rochester.

May 8, 2009
Status Conf.: USAO will not give 5K b/c no substantial assistance. And due to selling info, Watkins is not a credible cooperator.

July 2007 through March 2009: Watkins Proffers Info

July 13, 2009
Watkins files Motion to Enforce Plea Agreement. Alleges vindictive prosecution.

Jan. 29, 2010
Evidentiary Hearing. USAO presents witnesses: ATF, FBI, and OPR. Watkins testifies.

Sept. 29, 2010
Watkins moves to re-open the evidence to seek credit ▮▮

Jan. 23, 2011
Watkins moves to re-open the evidence to seek credit ▮▮

Feb. 10, 2012
The Court orders the Government to explain its decision not to file a 5K motion.

Spring 2010-Fall 2011: Watkins sells info to David Harvey & demands payment from Harvey's mother

Nov. 6, 2012
Government files pleading on 5K decision w/ Criminal Chief affidavit

May 8, 2013
Govt learns of Watkins selling info to David Harvey.

July 30, 2013
Court directs parties to advise whether a resolution has been reached.

Nov. 1, 2013
Status Conf. in chambers w/ J. Carnes. No resolution reached.

Dec. 19, 2013
Case referred for evidentiary hearing.

2009-Present: Watkins continues to send letters to the USAO

129

Exhibit D-6

1   MS. DAWSON: I DON'T HAVE ANY OBJECTION, YOUR HONOR.

2   THE COURT: ALL RIGHT.ADMITTED.

3   MR. PLUMMER: ALL RIGHT.

4   THE COURT: HE TRIED HARD, IN OTHER WORDS.

5   MR. PLUMMER: HE TRIED VERY HARD.HE EVEN CAME IN

6   LAST WEEK FOR THE PURPOSE OF BEING DEBRIEFED AND DURING THAT

7   TIME MR. HARVEY TOLD THE GOVERNMENT ABOUT A SCHEME INVOLVING

8   THE SELLING OF 5K AND RULE 35 INFORMATION BY AN INDIVIDUAL

9   KNOWN AS MR. WATKINS AND THAT—

10   THE COURT: HOW RECENTLY DID HE TELL YOU ALL THAT?

11   MR. PLUMMER: LAST WEEK.

12   WHAT DAY WAS THAT?

13   THE COURT: THAT IS MY MR. WATKINS? THAT IS MY.

14   MARCUS WATKINS?

15   MS. DAWSON: YES

16   MR. PLUMMER: YES, YES

17   AND SO, AS THE COURT CAN IMAGINE, THAT IS STILL IN

18   THE INVESTIGATORY DETERMINATION.IT'S TOO EARLY TO DETERMINE

19   WHETHER OR NOT THAT WOULD CONSTITUTE SUBSTANTIAL ASSISTANCE.

20   BUT DURING THE COURSE OF THAT DEBRIEFING IT IS ALSO MY

21   UNDERSTANDING THAT MR, HARVEY ADMITTED PURCHASING INFORMATION

22   WHICH HE, DURING THE COURSE OF THE EXHIBITS THAT THE COURT HAS

23   BEFORE IT AS EXHIBITS 1 THROUGH 9, SOME OF THAT INFORMATION IS

24   INFORMATION THAT HE ACTUALLY PURCHASED FROM —

25   THE COURT: HE DIDN'T KNOW IT HIMSELF?

UNITED STATES DISTRICT COURT

1   MR. PLUMMER: -- FROM MR. WATKINS.THAT'S CORRECT.

2 AND HE ADMITTED THAT FACT WHEN HESAT IN THE DEBRIEFING. SO,

3 AS THE COURT CAN IMAGINE, WE ARE KIND OF IN A QUANDARY.

4   I AM MAKING THIS INFORMATION KNOWN TO THE COURT

5 PURSUANT TO THE GOVERNMENT'S DUTY TO ADVISE THE COURT OF ALL

6 THE COOPERATION THAT THE DEFENDANT HAS FURNISHED, BUT

7 TECHNICALLY I NEED TO ADVISE THE COURT AND MR. HARVEY.

8 TECHNICALLY HE IS IN VIOLATION OF THE PLEA AGREEMENT.

9   THE GOVERNMENT IS NOT SEEKING TO SET ASIDE THE PLEA

10 AGREEMENT, BECAUSE UNDER THE TERMS OF HIS PLEA AGREEMENT HE HAD

11 AN OBLIGATION TO COOPERATE BUT HE ALSO HAD AN OBLIGATION TO

12 COOPERATE TRUTHFULLY, AND THAT BASED ON HIS SUBSEQUENT

13 ADMISSION THAT HE IN FACT WAS SUPPLYING THE GOVERNMENT WITH

14 INFORMATION THAT HE DID NOT ACTUALLY HAVE KNOWLEDGE OF BUT HE

15 HAD ACTUALLY PURCHASE THIS INFORMATION, IT'S MY POSITION, AT

16 LEAST TODAY IN COURT, THAT HE WAS NOT ALWAYS TRUTHFULLY

17 FURNISHING INFORMATION AND THEREFORE IN BREACH OF THE PLEA

18 AGREEMENT.THAT LEAVES THE GOVERNMENT IN A QUANDARY, BECAUSE

19 OBVIOUSLY, WE WANT TO PURSUE THE CASE AGAINST MR. WATKINS, BUT

20 THEN WE HAVE --

21   THE COURT: MR. WATKINS ACTUALLY WILL -- I THINK I'M

22 GOING TO GIVE IT TO A MAGISRATE JUDGE. SO, THERE   WILL BE A HEARING ON

23 THINK, GOTTEN THE LAST BRIEF OF THE LONG MR. WATKINS SAGA AND

24 THERE WILL BE A HEARING. SO, THERE WILL BE A HEARING ON

25 MR. WATKINS AND YOU ARE SAYING YOU MIGHT USE HIM AT SUCH A

UNITED STATES DISTRICT COURT

1 HEARING OR YOU MIGHT NOT?

2   MR. PLUMMER: I DON'T KNOW.   I THINK THAT ESSENTIALLY

3 MR. HARVEY HAS TO SOME EXTENT IMPEACHED HIMSELF BASED ON HIS

4 CANDID ADMISSIONS TOWARD ME AND SO I AM NOT SURE WHETHER THE

5 GOVERNMENT IS GOING TO BE ABLE TO USE HIM OR NOT.   THAT IS

6 SOMETHING THAT WILL BE LEFT UP -- I MEAN IF IN FACT HE IS USED.

7 AND I WOULD EXPECT THAT PERHAPS --AND MS. SHANYA DINGLE IS

8 HERE—PERHAPS THE GOVERNMENT WILL COME BACK FOR A RULE 35.

9 BUT I DON'T GUARANTEE THAT, BECAUSE WHEN HE SAT DOWN, HE WAS

10 SUPPOSED TO PROVIDE TRUTHFUL INFORMATION AND IT'S COME TO OUR

11 ATTENTION THAT THE INFORMATION THAT HE PROVIDED WAS NOT IN FACT

12 TRUTHFUL.

13   THE COURT: AS IT TURNED OUT, THOUGH, HE WAS TRUTHFUL

14 TO YOU TO ADMIT HOW HE GOT THE INFORMATION; HE ACTUALLY WAS

15 HONEST ABOUT THAT?

16   MR. PLUMMER: BASED ON WHAT HAS BEEN RELATED TO ME IT

17 APPEARS THAT HE ACTUALLY WAS ABLE TO FURNISH SOME DOCUMENTARY

18 EVIDENCE THAT WOULD SUPPORT HIS OR CORROBORATE HIS CLAIM THAT

19 IN FACT, HE PURCHASED SOME OF THE INFORMATION.   IN PARTICULAR,

20 THERE ARE SOME LETTERS, I BELIEVE, BETWEEN MR. WATKINS AND

21 MR. HARVEY'S MOTHER THAT WOULD INDICATE THAT MR. WATKINS WAS

22 TRYING TO COLLECT MONEY FOR THE INFORMATION.

23   THE COURT: IS MR. WATKINS STILL TRYING TO SELL

24 INFORMATION AT THIS LATE DATE OR ARE WE TALKING ABOUT SOMETHING

25 MUCH OLDER?

UNITED STATES DISTRICT COURT

Episode XVII

Exposing the Hidden Face of Corruption — Substantial Assistance Revoked x 15

Three months after the July 29, 2014 Evidentiary Hearing (October 2014), I was again transported to Atl-USAO for the 15th and final debriefing. In attendance were two members of Atl-USAO, two Federal Law Enforcement Agents, my Attorney and I. Nearly two years after the launch of the USA Today story and also after the Atl-USAO repeatedly cited to the courts that my cooperation hadn't risen to the level of substantial assistance, it's duration surpassed the 60 minute mark. The subject matter was a murder plot to kill the DEA-DTAF II's supervising and arresting federal agent in Fed-case no. 1:12-CR-329-TCB-LTW which I had become knowledgeable of via private one-on-one conversations with the individual that was orchestrating the murder plot.

I testified to this fact making the federal agents and Atl-USAO representatives aware of federal detainee Pablo Camaney-Arzate's (#64154-019) secret use of an unauthorized telephone pin number belonging to another detainee to secretly communicate with external co-conspirators, undetected by FLEAs. Records exist at RADDF-Deyton which will easily uncover the fact that within an hour after I testified, the federal agents confirmed this secret orchestration. Those federal agents had the staff at the RADDF-Deyton place detainee Arzate on complete telephone restriction that lasted in excess of twelve months. So what does that tell you about my testimony...can we say credulous...uhmm, saved the life of a federal agent...oh and what about cutting off the means, preventing or at least impeding further similar criminal activity by detainee Arzate. You're welcome! You're welcome.

Hold up, wait a minute. Do I detect the absence of a Thank You?! You're kidding me, right? Okay, so after using the stated information for their benefit, the Atl-USAO representatives deemed my cooperation in the above matter as not being of **"Substantial Assistance"**?!! You got me fucked up! And you use this lame excuse of refusing to file a Sentence Reduction Motion on my behalf, am I getting this right? You can't even imagine the fury I felt in that moment. Remember the Rain Shower? I just needa cool down, but I think I'll ratchet up a notch. I'm not done yet.

Let's turn up. I'm switching gears and throttling the reader's focus to Fed-case no. 1:09-CR-94-TCB (United States V. Martino Dameco Allen). In the case of defendant Martino Dameco Allen, Atl-USAO filed for a sentence reduction after he provided what the government deemed substantial assistance based on Allen's cooperation on a similar case which was far less in severity than that of the criminal activity of defendant Arzate, and yet my contribution was deemed unworthy. Really? Check it out. Martino Allen snitched concerning defendant Artis Lisbon (case no. 1:10-CR-251) secretly using Allen's detainee telephone pin number unauthorized at RADDF-Deyton to communicate undetected with external sources for the purpose of Lisbon secretly conducting and continuing criminal activity on a far lesser scale. It just doesn't compute — it simply doesn't add up. This and other indisputable facts clearly substantiate that Atl-USAO's refusal to file a Sentence Reduction Motion on my behalf has a motive of unconstitutional vindictiveness and has no rational relation to any legitimate government end. It's foundation rests on the revenge that Atl-USAO longs for targeting me, the federal detainee that fucked them by **Exposing the Hidden Face of Corruption** .

Episode XVIII

25 Stacks — Snitching Pans Out — Strikes Gold

July 2015, I transacted my highest priced sale of information to a Korean federal detainee also housed in B-5 Segregated Housing Unit. At a cost of $25,000, actually offered by the Korean, I felt pretty accomplished and quite appreciative. The negotiations for the sale and purchase of the information used in my July 2015 sale of information was conducted during B-5 Segregated Housing Unit's recreation time outside in three fenced in recreation cages. The segregated cages are side by side and designed like the dog cages at an animal shelter.

When first approached by the Korean soliciting my help to get him out of the legal situation that he was in, I instantly became very suspicious of him and very alert, keen on everything and everyone surrounding me. I mean, the timing couldn't be shadier, given that it closely trailed the release of the publication of the USA Today Newspaper article and was during the climax of my beef with Atl-USAO. I was insanely cautious as well as conscious of my manner of conversation with this Korean even though I had numerous conversations and dealings with him pertaining to other issues. After the solicitation of my assistance in obtaining a 5k1.1 Sentence Reduction, I spent several weeks just basically feeling him out. I did my due diligence prior to the actual sale and purchase of the information.

The information was furnished to me by a mixture of sources, some obtained directly from my external sources and some furnished by federal agents through my external sources. I hooked a big fish and a bigger payday. I instructed my external sources to contact federal agents that I had previous dealings with and informed those agents that I needed some quality, hot off the press information. In July 2015, after acquiring all the sought-after information, we completed the transaction. However, after flooding his two high priced attorneys with the purchased information prior to making contact with the referred to federal agents, one of the two attorneys became suspicious of how his client had all of a sudden come in possession of this stellar quality information.

After investigating, validating his suspicions, his attorney learned that his client purchased the information from that guy posted on the front page of the most popular newspaper in the country, exposed snitching for the government! Need I say that the attorney had an "Aww shit fit?" In that moment, he wasted no time contacting US Marshals and the staff at RADDF-Deyton demanding separation of his client from "That Guy." Business is business, and luckily for me, by that time, the $25,000 had already been delivered and split with my external sources. Therefore, I could have cared less about the Korean client or his attorney. Business, that's all it will ever be with me.

My detainee account transactions verify the increased deposits during that time by Koreans in the free world. Former Warden Randy Tillman, a very good man and decent human being, and GEO can confirm that on July 31, 2015, I had one of my external sources deliver $1,300 of the $25,000 to a female staff member within the staff parking lot of RADDF-Deyton.

Episode XIX

Veneer Authenticity

In June 2016, a "Writ" was issued out of North Carolina for my appearance and testimony, regarding a court proceeding related to cooperation that I had previously provided to the government. As a result, GEO transported me from RADDF-Deyton to Atlanta Hartsfield-Jackson International Airport where I was placed in USMS custody. Shortly thereafter, I was flown via FBP aircraft to the Federal Transfer Center, located in Oklahoma City, Oklahoma where I was held over seven days (June 10, 2016 to June 17, 2016) before being flown to Raleigh, North Carolina once again via FBP aircraft.

After arriving in Raleigh, North Carolina, I was placed in the custody of the Farmville, Virginia Sheriff Department, then transported hours away to the Piedmont Regional Jail in Farmville, Virginia. Somehow, between June 10th and my June 17th arrival, the writ that brought me there had been lifted. Funny! No appearance for court testimony in North Carolina required. So, I guess it's back to RADDF-Deyton...well, at some point in time, anyway. I didn't leave the Piedmont Regional Jail until August 1, 2016 en route back to Atlanta and didn't arrive back at the RADDF-Deyton until August 5, 2016. Therefore, whereas I was held at the Piedmont Regional Jail over a month after the writ had been lifted and in desperate need of cash, I made the best of my time there by doing the one thing that I do best, selling information to those in need of my services.

In July 2016, I struck a $5,000-dollar deal for the sale and purchase of some information with a white, state level inmate that was facing the likelihood of spending the rest of his life in prison for committing some horrific crimes. Obviously, not being from the state of Virginia, I had no ties or connections there which the white guy was aware of. I had no information, nor could I obtain any information pertaining to Virginia or any crimes committed in Virginia, which he would certainly need to get a reduced prison sentence. Therefore, in order for me to get that $5,000 out of that guy, I had to resort to committing robbery by "veneer authenticity." It just fell in my lap. Call it a scam, call it a Ponzi scheme, a sham, but it really is what it is...veneer truth. I was paid in hundreds of dollars of commissary items, cash deposited to my inmate account, and postal money orders sent to my external sources (all traceable transactions minus commissary items).

Every day after striking the $5,000 deal with the white inmate, I stayed on the telephone for long periods of time pretending to gather information pertaining to crimes in Virginia. These crimes and I didn't know each other, nor were they familiar with anyone in my circle of sources back home. So, I fabricated the information with only a veneer layer of truth, actual crimes that I had seen on the local news in prior days in addition to providing him with fabricated information pertaining to crimes in the State of Virginia including unsolved murders that he could at least verify as being actual crimes committed. I also had my external sources provide me with googled information pertaining to the State of Virginia consisting of names of inner cities like the crime ridden Norfolk, street names, locations, names of key neighborhoods, and other useful information in an effort to strengthen the base material supporting the glossy sheen to the veneer surface.

The inmate never suspected that he was being robbed by veneer authenticity, and due to the nature of his heinous crimes, I could give zero fucks, not one ounce of remorse for my actions.

Episode XX

Corrupt "Knock and Talk" Drug Busts

Since the July 2016 sale of information as a result of my segregated housing condition, I didn't interact with anyone needing or wanting to purchase any information until August 2019. Had the opportunity presented itself prior, I would have definitely continued selling information. Maybe a bit surprisingly, the buying and selling of information in and of itself is not illegal, but there are illegal elements often introduced. However, I run a legitimate information selling operation that is very beneficial to all parties involved. Why would I want to shut down my successful operation when the government hadn't shut down its booming operation?!

The selling of information only becomes illegal when the seller instructs the buyer to lie to the government in any regards to the purchased information, when no government agency has knowledge of or involvement in the information selling, or when the information selling is not beneficial to the government. I have never instructed any of my customers to lie to the government in any respect pertaining to the purchased information, nor have I ever had to instruct any of my customers to lie to the government in the selling aspect. After each of my transactions to sell information, I have always referred my customers to the Federal Agent(s) that I had obtained the information from and/or those federal agents that are members of the inner circle. The buying and selling of information occurred before me, during my time, and will continue to occur long after me.

In regards to the use of the sold and purchased information that was used to carry out those corrupt "Knock-n-Talk" drug busts, that I made reference to earlier, it is a warrantless action taken by Law Enforcement Agents to gain entrance to a residence by speaking with someone on the inside of the residence. Conducted without a search warrant or an arrest warrant, the arresting agents had to establish some form of probable cause that magnified the residents' criminal or illegal conduct. That's where federal agents brought me into the picture.

On several occasions prior to conducting a "Knock-n-Talk" drug bust, federal agents furnished me with detailed information pertaining to the residence and individual(s) which were targeted, then instructed me to find a reliable source for the information. The end result of their actions always resulted with probable cause for the "Knock-n-Talk" being established, me making money from the sale of the information, and the buyer of the information receiving a 5k1.1 or Rule 35 Sentence Reduction. It has always been my strong belief that the federal agents conducting those corrupt practices had a financial motive and did in fact individually benefit financially after entering into the selected residences.

Given that I am now a retired, labeled, career criminal, there is no possible way for those federal agents to somehow convince me or get me to ever believe that upon arrival at those Hispanic residences, the occupant(s) just up and gave federal agents consent to enter and search their residence(s) without a search warrant, knowing what they might find. Furthermore, there is no possible way for the federal agents to somehow convince me or get me to ever believe that after taking the steps that they took to establish probable cause for corrupt "Knock-n-Talk" drug busts that, after entry, they all of a sudden decided to play by the book and didn't pocket a sizable portion of the confiscated cash.

To substantiate my beliefs and these claims, I now turn your attention to Fed-case number 1:12-CR-329-TCB-LTW, which is only one of many corrupt "Knock-n-Talk" drug busts. Even though I had no form of involvement in that case or other corrupt "Knock-n-Talk" drug busts, I am very knowledgeable of the corruption that occurred in this one. In this particular Fed-case 1:12-CR-329-TCB-LTW, on August 23, 2011, federal defendant Carlos Alfredo Arevalo (one of two defendants) was arrested by federal agents DEA Atlanta Field Division Task Force Group II (DEA-DTAF II) inside apartment L-8 at Dunwoody Glen Apartments, 6750 Peachtree Industrial Boulevard, Doraville, Georgia, resulting in the seizure of $93,054.00 in cash, seven (7) handguns, two (2) rifles, fourteen (14) kilograms of cocaine, eleven (11) kilograms of methamphetamine and point one (.1) kilograms of liquid methamphetamine.

However, due to the discovery of the corrupt and illegal tactics that were used by the DEA-DTAF II's supervising and arresting Federal Agent, whom was actively involved and overseeing that entire corrupt "Knock-n-Talk," in September 2014 (date the trial was to begin), federal prosecutors at the Atl-USAO had to drop all charges against Defendant Carlos Alfredo Arevalo and later dropped all of the charges against the other defendant charged in that case, Pablo Camaney-Arzate #64154-019.

If fact checked, you, the reader of this book, will learn that the DEA-DTAF II supervising and arresting Federal Agent actively involved and overseeing the corrupt "Knock-n-Talk" drug bust on August 23, 2011 was suspended thereafter for allegedly engaging in a sexual relationship with the female confidential informant that he used for the purpose of building his case against the defendants, obtaining authorization for wiretaps and establishing probable cause. Further, you will also learn that in an effort to conceal the above facts and other incriminating facts from the American public including the many victims of those corrupt "Knock-n-Talk" drug busts (current and former Federal Prison inmates/defendants in other Fed-cases), Atl-USAO requested and was granted by the court to place all documentation pertaining to that supervising agent's action and suspension "Under Seal".

On several occasions, defendant Pablo Camaney-Arzate #64154-019 in case No. 1:12-CR-329-TBC-LTW filed documentation with the court, seeking to get those "Sealed" documents "Unsealed." It was also alleged that prior to his suspension, this same supervising agent was using large sums of cash said to have been taken from residences that were the targets of the corrupt "Knock-n-Talk" drug busts to pay confidential informants to fabricate information that he in return submitted to judges in affidavits seeking to get authorization for wiretaps and establishing probable cause.

Recorded surveillance camera footage and housing records will confirm that, for several years, defendant/detainee Pablo Camaney-Arzate #64154-019 (case No. 1:12-CR-329-TBC-LTW) and I were not only housed a few doors from one another within the B-5 Segregated Housing Unit of RADDF-Deyton, but also that, on many occasions, Pablo and I went out for recreation together for the sole purpose of conversation with each other.

The first of many things that Pablo told me was that the reported $93,054.00 in cash found in apartment L-8 was but a fraction of what was confiscated. So, what did the agent do with the bulk of what was there? The supervising and arresting agent accounted for only a pinch of the cash confiscated at apartment L-8 on that August 23, 2011 corrupt "Knock-n-Talk" drug bust and was suspended. Given that the Federal Prosecutors of Atl-USAO were forced to drop all of the charges against the defendant, Pablo Camaney-Arzate #64154-019 in case No. 1:12-CR-329-TCB-LTW, it is hard to believe that such allegations were inaccurate.

Episode XXI

JUDGES Rule in Favor of Corruption

On June 17, 2019, I was placed back into the general population housing unit A-4 at RADDF-Deyton, amongst numerous federal detainees who were fresh off the streets, still in the pre-trial stage. Within a month after my return to the general population, I immediately got back to doing what I do best: Obtaining and selling vital information! By attempting to reconnect with several of the inner circle federal agents, I had worked with in the past. Initially I was frustrated and disappointed, when I reached out to the Federal Agents who once provided me with credible Intel to sell and they advised that I was damaged goods and no longer a use to them. WTF?! I am the M.V.P.! I'm the "King-Snitch of the South"; How in the fuck can I be of no use?

Pondering my next move and how I was going to find my way back into the inner circle, I would later discover that those same Federal Agents had replaced me and was providing salable information to several new cooperating federal detainees/defendants also being housed at the RADDF-Deyton along with myself. After crossing paths with a few of them, I readily realized they were not truly committed to the snitching game and not as effective as me.

On July 11, 2019, after years of waiting, the magistrate judge presiding over my motion to "Enforce the Plea Agreement" finally issued his Final Report and Recommendation to the higher judge presiding over my Fed-case recommending that my motion seeking to get the court to enforce the plea agreement be denied. It's evident that the magistrate judge based his recommendation on nothing but the government's word that my cooperation wasn't of substantial assistance instead of basing his recommendation on the actual evidence presented to the court that clearly substantiates the fact that my cooperation was of substantial assistance to the government. Not only does the evidence presented to the court substantiate my claims but so does the government's own actions in arranging a staggering number of debriefings with the same cooperating individual, i.e. 15! Otherwise, it's simply a waste of time, money and energy, and that just wasn't their MO.

Therefore, the most reasonable explanation for the government debriefing me a total of 15 times lends itself to the very possibility that I had what they wanted, and in my coughing up the goods, they always prevailed, because I was, in fact, providing useful, consistent, "substantial assistance." Furthermore, any person of reasonable intelligence and logic would be able to deduce that had I not been helpful to the government, there would have been far fewer than 15 iterations of debriefings.

In September 2019, my attorney filed an objection to the magistrate judge's entire Final Report and Recommendation which, on September 24, 2019, the higher judge presiding over my Fed-case quickly overruled, citing that under the law as it stands, the decision of whether or not to file a 5k1.1 or Rule 35 Sentence Reduction Motion rests solely with the USAO.

In other words, what the two judges presiding over my Fed-case are saying and have allowed to happen is that Atl-USAO under the false pretense of filing a 5k1.1 or Rule 35 Sentence Reduction Motion on behalf of the cooperating individual cannot only debrief an individual on numerous occasions pertaining to a variety of different individuals and topics of interests but also use that individual's cooperation and provided information to the benefit of the USAO and then under the law as it now stands and at their discretion, refuse to file a 5k1.1 or Rule 35 Sentence Reduction Motion on behalf of that individual.

I was scheduled to be sentenced on January 29, 2020. Surprise, I was pushed off again and held up during Covid 19 restrictions. As of October 2019, I was back to work selling beneficial information. One of the most important things that I have learned, witnessing myself on numerous occasions, and now being victimized by the same is that whenever the evidence is favorable to the defendant, 99% of the time, the court will agree with federal prosecutors or somehow assist federal prosecutors in coming out on top, no matter what the circumstances may be or no matter what the evidence points to. Once again, I say to you that the entire Federal Court System is corrupt.

Episode XXII

Our Legal Justice System — Criminal at its Roots

So now, I've taken the liberty to enlighten the American Public of the details of our corrupt government's role in a twisted "Criminal Information Selling Scheme" possibly affecting someone close to you even as you read this novel. I come clean, taking ownership in my corporate role as I am a seller of information 'planted' in my brain by the very prosecutor sending your loved ones, friends and acquaintances to prison for life, guilty or not, but certainly inadmissible evidence whether planted, illegally obtained, or tainted. Our justice system is criminal at its roots.

This corrupt practice takes away the grace of our justice system 'so help me God' and is happening as your eyes scan over my words. (Those who psychologically live in a perfect bubble and view life in the same aspect will never believe any of what I've shared to be true, even though the evidence is physically in black and white.)

This quid pro quo setup is a vicious cycle of offering info, fabricating info, soliciting info from outside, then selling to buyers, the prospective recipients of the sentence reduction, presenting the info purchased back to the agency that is the origin of the info in the first place, then an agreement to testify to that info brought back to the originator; then to complete the quid pro quo, conviction, sentencing then reduction of sentence. How can anyone follow that?!! What's really going on? So, you're telling me that "The Originator" seeks a convicted felon to buy the information, return it to them, the Feds, then testify in hopes of getting a reduced sentence? Is that what you see? If so, you're probably blinded, but certainly not blind — it's a well oiled scheme of corruption!

This scheme is actively occurring in the city of Atlanta (actually all 50 States if not around the world as long as the USAO is concerned) at the publication of this book. Please don't misconstrue these facts with the belief that the selling of information is only occurring in Atlanta. With so many individuals wanting, needing, and seeking to obtain sentence reductions, I can assure you that there is a market for the purchasing of salvation enticing information in every city and state.

The Federal 5k1.1 and Rule 35 Sentence Reduction Laws weren't put into existence to just be utilized by individuals in Atlanta with Federal charges. They were put into existence to be utilized by every individual (male/female) with federal charges in every city and state transcontinental and satellite states. Furthermore, it is a proven fact that federal agents and Federal Prosecutors don't really care how the information is obtained as long as the information is accurate and useful to the government. The December 14, 2012 USA Today Newspaper article that I was featured in quoted FBI Agent Miles Brosas stating during 2010 court testimony that Agents executed, "just based on the names that Mr. Watkins gave us" (Revisit the USA Today Newspaper article).

The selling of information is such a lucrative business that I've actually witnessed other information sellers go to the extreme of instructing their external sources to plant evidence, such as several ounces of crack cocaine and a firearm at a specific location at a cost of no more than $2000 to the information seller. But then the seller turns around and sells the knowledge of the location and some false information pertaining to the ounces of crack cocaine and the firearm to a buyer at a price much higher than that of the $2000 invested by the information seller. Once the goods are in place, the information seller can then provide the buyer with any type of supporting information that the information seller wishes to provide, because the goods can then be found at the exact location that the information seller provides to the buyer.

With there being so many methods that can be utilized to obtain a 5k1.1 or Rule 35 Sentence Reduction, such activity is to be expected. Furthermore, as of the writing of this book, other than the David Joe Harvey and Korean customer situations which were neither a result of mine and federal agents' modus operandi, my success rate in regards to my customers obtaining the sought-after 5k1.1 or Rule 35 Sentence Reduction using purchased information is 100%. I have never failed to deliver the goods, and how could I fail with corrupt federal agents furnishing me with the goods and having them on my side? That would be an oxymoron.

In fact, obtainable legal documentation from the sentencing hearing of one of my customers, Leon Lumsden charged with white collar crimes, will validate that he received a 5k1.1 Sentence Reduction even greater than proposed by Federal Prosecutors. It will also verify that federal agents came to the sentencing hearing and lauded Leon's cooperative efforts in the face of the sentencing judge.

With or without my involvement, the selling of information will continue and has continued. There will always be a market for quality information. The overall game/hustle of snitching has become such a common thing in today's society. The code of the street is only honored when in the presence of self, because behind closed doors and when your freedom is at state the only honor upheld is "SNITCHING."

Episode XXIII

King Snitch of the South Unseals 5k1.1 Loophole

In regards to those that have purchased information having to testify as to credible evidence supporting the subject matter of the purchased information, the percentage of defendants entering plea agreements are disproportionately higher than those that actually take their federal court case to trial. The buyer must be prepped to testify in court proceedings regarding the purchased information resulting almost always in the award of either a 5K1.1 or Rule 35 Sentence Reduction for the buyer.

However, when the target of the sold information decides to go to trial within days of the court proceedings, Federal Prosecutors and Federal Agents spend relentless time prepping buyers (snitching witnesses). Regardless, a key prep focus is the witnesses' response to the inevitable question by the defense attorney's cross examination of the buyer, "Isn't it true that the government has promised you a 5K1.1 or Rule 35 Sentence Reduction for your (snitch/witness) testimony today against my client (target/defendant)?" The snitch is prepared to respond, "No. The government hasn't promised me anything for my testimony." Now you know that's perjury, a slick-faced lie.

Cleverly, the plea agreement that federal prosecutors have cooperating snitches sign clearly states that the government "may" file a 5K1.1 or Rule 35 Sentence Reduction on behalf of that individual after the completion of his/her cooperation, therefore the government doesn't promise in writing that the individual "will" be awarded a 5K1.1 or Rule 35 Sentence Reduction. Thus, the keyword, "may," buys the government a loophole for this question on the cross examinations of cooperating government (snitch) witness.

With such short fuse trials, it's easy to see that the strategic prepping is out, and tactical prep is in. There are many methods which can be utilized to obtain a 5k1.1 or Rule 35 Sentence Reduction, and there is also a very high percentage of sentence reductions being obtained using purchased information. To stop the buying and selling of information completely, the government would have to do away with its 5k1.1 and Rule 35 Sentence Reduction laws, which will never happen, no matter how many times the defense attorney cross examines the buyer with this question of award.

The Federal Court System and FBP in one way or another both revolve around "snitching." Without those that have "snitched" and/or those that will "snitch" in the decades to come, the Federal court system, the FBP, and my information selling operation would all be out of business, and I can assure you that neither of us are going to ever allow that to happen.

The simplistic principle of supply and demand always governs. As such, there will always be demand for worthy information, so there will always be a supply channel to afford those in need the opportunity to purchase quality information. With or without my involvement, the selling of information will continue. And the beat goes on. Like an Atlanta Falcon or Hawk hovering over its prey, my eyes and ears are on high alert for something beneficial. I am the "KING-Snitch of the South" and will continue to honor my title as long as there's a personal gain.

Exhibit E-1

Case 1:06-cr-00442-TCB-AJB   Document 207   Filed 02/25/16   Page 1 of 2

IN THE UNITED STATES DISTRICT COURT
FOR THE NORTHERN DISTRICT OF GEORGIA
ATLANTA DIVISION

UNITED STATES OF AMERICA,   :

                            :   CRIMINAL INDICTMENT

                            :   NO. **1:06-CR-442-TCB-AJB**

v.   :

                            :

MARCUS WATKINS,   :

MOTION TO UNSEAL ENTIRE RECORD

COMES NOW Marcus Watkins, defendant above named and moves this

Court by and through undersigned counsel to unseal the entire record in his case.

Respectfully submitted this the 25th day of February 2016.

/s/ *William A. Morrison*

William A. Morrison
State Bar #525186
Attorney for Marcus Watkins

Jones, Morrison & Womack, P.C.
101 Marietta Street, Suite 3175
Atlanta, Georgia 30303
Phone: 404-658-1670
Fax: 404-584-5994
bmorrison@jonesmorrison.com

150

CERTIFICATE OF SERVICE

I hereby certify that I have on this date electronically filed a **MOTION TO UNSEAL ENTIRE RECORD** with the Clerk of Court using the CM/ECF system, which will automatically send e-mail notification of such filing to all parties of record in this case.

Respectfully submitted this the 25th day of February 2016.

/s/ *William A. Morrison*
William A. Morrison
State Bar #525186
Attorney for Marcus Watkins

To the Readers:

Dear Readers,

I can assure you that all the contents of this book are true and accurate. Whereas some or even all of you may not agree with my actions, and the incarcerated readers may feel as though I'm glorifying "snitching," I leave you with the following two statements.

First, we know from Solomon that there is nothing new under the sun. I haven't done anything that millions of other individuals haven't already done, aren't currently involved in, or will not do in the near future.

Secondly, no matter how you look at or interpret my actions, at the end of the day, it's just business. I'm very much aware that the publication of this book will expose the world to my selfishness and cause my life to be in even greater jeopardy, but I honestly feel it's time the truth is told.

Need I say more?

Marcus Watkins
#46440-019

www.ingramcontent.com/pod-product-compliance
Lightning Source LLC
Chambersburg PA
CBHW080050280326
41934CB00014B/3267